ESSAYS

COMMUNICATION &

SPIRITUALITY

Contributions to a
New Discourse on Communication

Edited by
Amardo Rodriguez

University Press of America,® Inc.
Lanham · New York · Oxford

Copyright © 2001 by
University Press of America,® Inc.
4720 Boston Way
Lanham, Maryland 20706

12 Hid's Copse Rd.
Cumnor Hill, Oxford OX2 9JJ

Library of Congress Cataloging-in-Publication Data

Essays on communication & spirituality : contributions to a
new discourse on communication / edited by Amardo Rodriguez.
p.   cm
Includes bibliographical references.
1. Communication—Religious aspects. 2. Spiritual life. I. Title:
Essays on communication and spirituality. II. Rodriguez, Amardo.

P94 .E74 2001   291.1'75—dc21   2001041482 CIP

ISBN 0-7618-2079-5 (pbk. : alk. paper)

This book is dedicated to those who believe in the potentiality of communication to make for a better world.

Table of Contents

v

Acknowledgements

Many persons contributed to the completion of this book. We would like to thank Patrice Buzzanell, Bill Rawlins, Chuck Morris, and Patty Hawk for reading and commenting on many of the essays in this volume. We are especially grateful to Julie Morris and Sherrill Miller for carefully reading the complete manuscript. We would also like to thank our families, friends, and colleagues for their support of our work.

The Nature Of Our Contribution

Amardo Rodriguez
Syracuse University

Our goal in this book is to offer a collection of essays that expands our understanding of communication theory and inquiry. We aim to present in one volume beginning positions in an emerging discourse in the communication field. Specifically, all of these essays explore the potential contribution of work premised on assumptions of the salience of spirituality for the study of communication. The essays also examine and illustrate how scholarly work that is premised on such spiritual assumptions reshapes our understanding of communication.

This book therefore demonstrates how explicitly acknowledging spiritual assumptions might expand our conversations about communication. Although all the contributors work with a different definition of spirituality, we all assume that human beings are fundamentally and inherently spiritual beings. We believe that this assumption significantly alters and broadens our understanding of communication theory in many important and significant ways.

First, to view human beings as spiritual beings allows us to understand better what being human means. It enlarges our comprehension of the human condition by deepening our view of the complexity that accompanies human endeavors. In acknowledging spirituality as part of who we are, we find a level of complexity that is rarely recognized in communication theory and inquiry. A spiritual view of communication pushes us to develop more encompassing understandings and theories of communication and what being human means.

Second, to look at human beings as spiritual beings deepens our understanding of the nature of communication and the relation between communication and being human. We no longer assume, as dominant understandings of communication casually do, that the origins and purposes of communication reside in necessity and utility. Instead, we assume that communication manifests and articulates our spirituality. That is, communication uniquely defines us. It distinctively reflects our beauty, complexity, and spirituality. To communicate is to manifest our ability and potentiality to have a different relation to the world.

Third, to view human beings as spiritual beings expands the potentiality of communication to help make for a new and better world. In expanding our understanding of the human condition and giving us new understandings of communication, this view gives us new vistas of our relationality and, in so doing, encourages us to foster more life-affirming ways of being in the world with others. In other words, a spiritual view of communication helps us to forge new and different conceptions of ethics, democracy, diversity, and community. It enlarges the realm of possibilities.

Finally, in expanding and redefining communication theory, acknowledging spirituality makes for a more inclusive communication theory by giving recognition and legitimacy to voices that have been too long marginalized and disenfranchised in communication theory. A secular hegemony pervades communication theory that makes for an overly narrow definition of communication and, consequently, a shallow understanding of what being human means. More importantly, however, this secular hegemony makes for a pernicious form of colonialism. In reinforcing a secular view of the world, this hegemony privileges one set of beliefs, values, assumptions, hopes, and truths, that is, one worldview. As a consequence, communication inquiry is overwhelmingly of one epistemology. We hope that this book undermines the colonialism that this secular hegemony perpetuates. We strive for a more inclusive and expansive communication theory and inquiry.

We are extremely excited about this book. The essays in this book reflect different theoretical and pedagogical areas of study (e.g., interpersonal, organizational, rhetorical) in the communication field. Also, the essays are highly readable as this book is intended for different kinds of audiences.

We believe that our book offers the theoretical range to become required reading for scholars and students interested in the evolution of this quickly emerging discourse on communication and spirituality. We know of no other book in the communication field that addresses this subject. We are confident that the essays in this volume will appeal greatly to scholars and students who often complain about the absence of this kind of project.

Chapter 1

The Co-Construction Of Self And Organization: Evoking Organizational Spirituality

Diane F. Witmer
California State University, Fullerton

Abstract

This chapter reconceptualizes organizational culture as characterized by organizational spirituality, and explores ways in which human agents interact with self and others to evoke organizational spirituality and recursively create both organization and self. Adopting a structurationist perspective, the essay focuses on Alcoholics Anonymous to illustrate the ways in which individual and organizational communication practices enact an organizational spirituality that can bring to presence personal spirituality, healing, and recovery. I outline the characteristics and features of organizational spirituality, and suggests some ways in which spirituality might emerge in organizations other than Alcoholics Anonymous. Finally, I propose some suggestions for future communication research in organizations that includes spirituality as a feature of organizational culture.

A s organizational communication scholars look toward the
future, serious questions arise concerning the nature and
substance of organizations in the twenty-first century, and the ways in
which they must operate in a postmodern realm. Mitroff, Mason, and
Pearson (1994) declared that the world is undergoing a revolution as
"profound as that from the Agrarian to the Industrial Age," (p. 11) which
requires a re-thinking of today's obsolete nineteenth- and twentieth-century
organizations.

A growing body of research recognizes that the concept of the
rational organization discounts fundamental relational needs (e.g., Mumby
& Putnam, 1992), ambiguities (e.g., Meyerson, 1991), issues of gender
and equality (e.g., Pringle, 1989), and human capability for both good and
evil acts (e.g., Fox, 1994). The culture metaphor, while useful, fails to
address some aspects of human interactions in organizations, and of the
relationship that mutually constructs the self and the organization. One
approach that can resolve some of these difficulties is the consideration of
human beings as spiritual beings who are creators and creations of
organizations.

This chapter focuses on Alcoholics Anonymous, in order to explore
the ways in which individual and organizational communication practices
enact an organizational spirituality. AA offers a rich field for studying
organizational life and the relationships between human actors and the
organization. Both AA and its members operate across blurred cultural
borders. They function within and through social, geographic,
professional, and organizational cultures that tend to both valorize and
stigmatize alcohol abuse. Thus, its cultural situation places AA and its
members in the "borderlands," where "meaning is contested and struggled
for in the interstices" (Conquergood, 1991, p. 184).

Adopting a structurationist approach, this essay outlines the
characteristics and features of organizational spirituality, describes the
spiritual culture that AA members socially construct through their
communication practices. and suggests some ways in which spirituality
might emerge in organizations other than Alcoholics Anonymous. Finally,
it proposes possible directions for future communication research in
organizations. The next sections of this essay review the literature on
spirituality, and demonstrate the centrality of human interaction to
organizational life.

Scholarship on Spirituality

While matters of the spirit are traditionally considered to be in the domain of theologians and religious scholars, the concept of spirituality is gaining recognition as an aspect of human experience that is worthy of study by psychiatrists and psychologists (e.g., Madhere, 1993; Morgan & Cohen, 1994; Prasinos, 1992; Schneider, 1993; Valentine & Feinauer, 1993; Vaughan, 1991; Waldram, 1993; Watts, 1993; Witmer & Sweeney, 1992), the medical community (e.g., Diaz, Caplan, & Mauer, 1993; McKee & Chappel, 1992; Reed, 1993; Resnick, Harris & Blum, 1993; Schmidt, 1993), criminologists (e.g., Palermo, Simpson, Knudten, Turci, & Davis, 1993), social workers (e.g., Sheridan, Bullis, Adcock, Berlin, & Miller, 1992), educators (e.g., Weaver & Cotrell, 1992), and political and social scientists (e.g., Albanese, 1993; McGuire, 1993; Roof, 1993). However, communication scholars are taking matters of the spirit seriously, as well. Pym (1997) proposes that ethics in the postmodern era must be grounded in Spirit, rather than in rational consensus. Smith (1993) recognizes spirituality as central to transcendence, and Kirkwood (1994) stresses the importance of studying both communication about spirituality and the spiritual consequences of communication. Tukey (1995), while diverging from Kirkwood's views, considers the study of spirituality necessary for addressing concerns about human development.

Goodall (1993) believes the trend toward spirituality is an intellectual response to the problems of everyday living, and that it addresses the difficulties raised by the deconstructions of postmodernism. He places spirituality squarely at the center of communication studies, and asks, "What would a theory of communication include if we took seriously the idea that humans are, first and foremost, spiritual beings?" (p. 41). The question articulates a key proposal of this essay: that people are spiritual beings, and that organizations manifest the spirituality of the humanity that creates them, works through them, and plays within them.

Scholarly works that address the realm of the spirit offer a variety of definitions for spirituality, and the distinctions between spirituality and religion often are blurred (e.g., Albanese, 1993; Ellis & Schoenfeld, 1990; Sheridan, Bullis, Adcock, Berlin, & Miller, 1992; Zimmerman & Maton, 1992). Other works approach spirituality from mystical and largely nonconsensual perspectives (e.g., Albanese, 1993, Csikszentmihalyi, 1993; Frohock, 1993; Madhere, 1993; Roof, 1993, Weaver and Cotrell, 1992).

Hawley (1993) attempts to define spirituality, particularly in contrast to religion, with some limited success. To him, spirituality is beyond body, mind, thoughts, feelings, passions, memories, or innate tendencies (Hawley, 1993, p. 16). Spirituality, for Hawley, is the goal; religion is the path. Spirituality moves the individual from uncertainty to clarity; it is an inquiry into "true Self," whereas religion involves sets of beliefs, rituals, and ceremonies (p. 4). To Goodall (1993), spirituality is ineffable. Although a number of other communication scholars have talked *around* spirituality, or described *aspects* of spirituality (e.g., Bineham, 1989; Hikins, 1989; Scott, 1989; Tukey, 1989), its features, particularly as related to organizations, has yet to be explicated.

Based on theological and religious scholarship, Pokora (1996) proposes a typology for describing various aspects of spirituality. While not mutually exclusive, her four categories provide a useful articulation of the concept of spirituality. The first category is incorporeal spirituality, which Jones, Wainwright, and Yarnold (1986) consider to be "distinct from things of matter," (p. xxiv). Pokora's second category is a totalizing spirituality, which considers spirituality as encompassing life, and as the means through which Religion is manifested in all human action. The third category links faith and action, and the fourth category proposes that spirituality offers individual paths to developing a "closer relationship with the divine" (p. 20).

This essay proposes that people are imbued with incorporeal spirituality that also is totalizing, because it is discursively enacted throughout organizational life by spiritual human actors. Thus, through organizational and individual communicative practices, an organizational spirituality is brought to presence. To explore the phenomenon in the AA organization, this article focuses on the social interactions that create and are created by human agency within the AA context, as propounded in Giddens' structuration (Giddens, 1976; 1979; 1981; 1984), and draws upon the conceptualizations of Bateson (1972) and Denzin (1987a; 1987b, 1988), who explored the ways in which the alcoholic self is transformed through recovery.

Structuration Theory

Giddens proposes that human agency is the functioning of stocks of knowledge; people know how to proceed in social interactions based on mutually understood norms and learning experiences. Self-reflexivity of individuals allows them to articulate goals and motivations, although not all human action is consciously motivated (Giddens, 1984). The rules and resources people use in social interaction are structures, and there are three basic types: legitimation (normative action), domination (allocation or authorization of resources), and signification (symbolic action; language). Duality of structure is an aspect of structuration that is particularly important to this essay, in that "the structural properties of social systems are both the medium and outcome of the practices they recursively organize" (Giddens, 1984, p. 25). This structurationist perspective enables the researcher to see the organizational spirituality of AA as it is recursively constituted by spiritual actors.

Alcoholics Anonymous and Spirituality

The program of Alcoholics Anonymous is grounded in spiritually-based tenets that claim "spiritual progress rather than spiritual perfection" (*Alcoholics Anonymous*, 1976, p. 60), concepts that align most closely with Pokora's (1996) classification of path spirituality. The AA approach to spirituality has drawn attention from both scholars (e.g., Carroll, 1993; Galanter, 1990; Hanna, 1992; Heise, 1991; Prezioso, 1986; Uva, 1991) and popular press (e.g., Gelman, Leonard & Fisher, 1991; Stein, 1988). Heise and Steitz (1991) consider the broad AA concept of spirituality superior to fundamentalist Christian perfectionism, which (echoing Kenneth Burke) they declare to be counterproductive for the imperfect individual in recovery. Their work, though, like that of many authors (e.g., Brizer, 1993; Stafford, 1991), seems to muddle the distinction between spirituality and the more synthetic construct of religion. AA's co-founder, Bill Wilson, while acknowledging a monotheistic foundation, drew a clear differentiation between spirituality and religion in a 1954 letter:

> Beyond a Higher Power, as each of us may vision Him, AA must never, as a society, enter the field of dogma or theology. We can never become a religion in that sense, lest we kill our usefulness by getting bogged down in theological contention (*As Bill Sees It*, 1967, p 116).

This spirituality was evident in an ethnographic study by the author (Witmer, 1997). That research indicated that the AA discourse was sprinkled liberally with quotations from charismatic leaders, the Twelve Steps (*Twelve Steps*, 1953), the Twelve Traditions (*Twelve Steps*, 1953), and the "Big Book" (*Alcoholics Anonymous*, 1976), all of which espoused belief in a God of personal understanding and a focus on spirituality. The structures of legitimation, signification, and domination both created and were created by members who told their stories, reordering their lives and perceptions of self, in dyadic conversations and telephone calls, informal group discussions over dinner or coffee, and as speakers in meetings. Structures of signification (symbolic action; language) addressed a Power greater than the members themselves (e.g., *Alcoholics Anonymous*, 1976). Structures of legitimation (normative action) reinforced and celebrated personal transcendence, sobriety, action, and service to a greater good.

Both the language of the members and their social interactions carried with them acknowledgment of a Higher Power, of selflessness and altruism as means for recovery, and of personal and collective spirituality and transcendent action through prayer and meditation. Finally, structures of domination (allocation or authorization of resources) invested organizational resources toward social responsibility, within the realm of recovery from alcoholism.

These findings are congruent with the scholarly literature across disciplines that shows, despite the fuzziness surrounding spirituality versus theology, a clear consistency in recognizing linkages between spirituality and physical or emotional healing, a connectedness with things spiritual throughout AA, and the effectiveness of the organization in facilitating recovery. This indicates recovery for AA members is grounded in a spiritual development that requires a profound ontological and epistemological shift from the alcoholic self to the recovering self.

Alcoholics Anonymous and the Recovering Self

Rudy & Greil (1988) describe AA as an Identity Transformation Organization (ITO) that envelops its members and encourages in them "radical shifts of worldview," (p. 46) much as a cocoon protects its contents from interference during the process of metamorphosis (p. 46). This concept of transformation is congruent with Bateson's assertion that members of Alcoholics Anonymous undergo "a change in epistemology, a change in how to know about the personality-in-the-world" (Bateson, 1972, p. 313). Denzin (1987a) draws on the works of William James (whose writings also influenced the AA founders and the AA literature), Berger and Luckmann (1967), Burke (1954), Strauss (1959), Thune (1977), Travisano (1981, pp. 242-244), and Wallace (1982), to identify the process as a "radical transformation of personal identity that signals a conversion and commitment to a new way of life" (p. 168). Certainly, sober AA members manifest new behaviors, express fresh or reclaimed values, and develop personal relationships (Witmer, in press). The result is that the recovering alcoholic "undergoes a radical transformation of self" (Denzin, 1987a, p. 168).

Denzin (1987a, p. 130) calls alcoholism a "dis-ease with the world that is temporal, relational, and emotional," and posits that the alcoholic "acquires a new language of self... a new set of meanings concerning alcohol, alcoholism, alcoholics, and the drinking act. By becoming a part of the lived history of AA the individual is transformed into a 'recovering alcoholic' within a society of fellow alcoholics" (p. 168). Even as the recovering alcoholic becomes part of the AA culture, he or she is disunited from "the larger society that continues to sanction the cultural and interactional use of alcohol on a regular basis" (Denzin, 1987a, p. 168). Thus, in striving for sobriety and maintaining abstinence from alcohol, the alcoholic adopts a way of life that is not congruent with the life he or she once saw as "normal," and which a larger society condones. By committing to recovery, the alcoholic eschews what is seen as normal outside Alcoholics Anonymous. He or she identifies as a recovering alcoholic, embracing the identity proscribed and symbolically reinforced within the organization. Thus, recovering selves are created and recreated, as they enact and create organizational structures. The self and the organization is co-constructed.

AA structures constitute and characterize an organizational spirituality that recursively instills in the transmutational self stocks of knowledge that allow abstinence from alcohol, even as the spirituality is brought to presence by the interactions of alcoholic selves. At the same time, the social constructions of the members both constrain and emancipate the alcoholic self, offering protection from an unsympathetic world, freedom from self-destructive choices, and the clearing for ontological transformation. It is an evocation of, rather than a construction of, human spirituality.

Organizational Spirituality

In the social interactions within AA, a collective of spiritual beings creates collective spirituality, an extension of the culture metaphor that might be called organizational spirituality. Acknowledging spirituality in organizations is a rediscovery of the spiritual nature of human beings. In organizational cultures, it is something one senses throughout upon entering a room or through interactions with organizational members. Considering such a spirituality in Alcoholics Anonymous and the ways in which the founding influences and communicative practices create and perpetuate it, may enable the exploration of the lived but unarticulated aesthetic, emotional, ethical, and intuitive aspects of the "webs of significance" (Geertz, 1973, p. 5) that are woven by and between organizational actors. Spirituality affects the organizational climate, influences organizational norms, and is a significant part of the recovery process for AA members.

Characteristics and Features of Organizational Spirituality

In the AA context, spirituality is understood as a personally-defined state of being (e.g., *Alcoholics Anonymous*, 1976); its specifics are determined by matters of faith, and it most closely aligns with Pokora's (1996) classification of path spirituality. Because AA is grounded in Western Christianity, it often is articulated as monotheistic, but it encompasses all faiths and religions, and it is more visceral than dogmatic. This indicates that spirituality is a precursor to religion rather than a construction of it, although religious and charismatic groups may bring spirituality to presence.

In order for the concept of organizational spirituality to inform scholarly research, it is important to tease the concepts of *religiosity*, spiritual *belief* and matters of *faith* from the snarled literature. The question is not whether human agents believe in a God, or gods, or oneness with nature, or hobgoblins, nor whether the religious path is Christian, Buddhist, Druid, or Wiccan, but that there is some power that is greater than mere humanity, and that a noncorporeal essence imbues humanness. Human understanding or acknowledgment of that power does not create it, nor does human denial destroy it. It simply *is*. It is this concept (which AA calls a Higher Power) that distinguishes the construct of spirituality from pagan humanism.

The organizational issue, particularly in relationship to AA, is one of acknowledging that human agents are spiritual beings, that there is some power to which humanity is connected beyond that of the individual, and of coming to some understanding of what it means to be spiritual. If one pursues the concept of human spirituality as manifested in Alcoholics Anonymous, it seems clear that human collectivity can bring to presence a collective spirituality. This leads to questions of how the concept of organizational spirituality be extended to encompass other organizations. Engineering or aerospace or microelectronics firms, for example, seem to manifest little discernible organizational spirituality. What are the implications if organizational members deny human spirituality? The answer, of course, is that denial of something does not extirpate its existence.

Spirituality and Piety in Organizations

The review of the literature indicates that spirituality is alive and well in the late modern era. In AA, this connection is relatively easy to see. It is manifest in the organizational discourse and in the personal recovery of organizational members. The question, then, becomes one of how spirituality emerges in other organizations. People vary widely in belief systems and values, and not all organizations evince an overtly spiritual bias. Alcoholics Anonymous, then, might be called "spiritually enriched," because organizational members are enthusiastic and intense in their expression of spirituality, their values, and their organizational goals. They cohere and make collective sense of deeply layered structures that span space and time. This sense-making acknowledges and ultimately celebrates human spirituality in order to capitalize on it for personal betterment and organizational survival.

The assumption that culture is something an organization *is* rather than something an organization *has* (Riley, 1983) points to the idea that transcendent collective action may stem not from temporal collectivity, but rather from the inherent spirituality of organizational members. While organizing creates the opportunity, collective human spirituality synergistically enables recovery for individuals. AA might be considered "spiritually enriched," because it unabashedly nurtures the spirituality of its members and its organizational culture. Other organizations, however, suppress or deny the spirituality of their human constituents. These organizations might be called "spiritually deprived," because spirituality is relegated to invisibility, where only the bottom-line, "left-brained," "just-the-facts-ma'am" sorts of things are recognized or valued at the institutional level. Even here, though, isolated pockets or moments of irrepressible spirituality can emerge. The dynamic assembly team, the stellar fund-raising committee, and the wildly creative advertising group all embody the abstraction.

The concepts of spiritual enrichment or deprivation, while polar opposites, do not constitute a true dichotomy, but rather opposing ends of a continuum, and they are independent of the belief systems of organizational constituents. The notion refers only to the extent to which spirituality is palpable through individual and organizational artifacts and exigencies. Acknowledging spirituality in organizations requires trust, as well as a shift in traditional ideas of managerial power and control (an idea already emerging, for example, in self-managed work teams). Spiritual "enrichment" or "deprivation," however, should not be confused with opinions of faith.

Organizations, like their human agents, manifest systems of belief and systems of faith. Alcoholics Anonymous is what might be called a "pious" organization. Its members are overtly spiritual, and speak openly of their spirituality in terms of God or a Higher Power, and of recovery grounded in spiritually-based action. Collectively, the human agents create and recreate themselves and their organization, spinning communicative cocoons that envelop and, ultimately, transform their conceptions of self as non-drinkers and as spiritual beings. Faith in a Higher Power, however, is not a requirement for organizational spirituality. An organization and its constituents may be agnostic or even atheistic (e.g., agnostic groups of AA, which deny that acknowledgment of a "Higher Power" is necessary for recovery, or symphony orchestras, which practice mathematically-based musicianship to create artistry and music). Organizational "agnosticism" or "piety," then, refer to the constitutive beliefs and value systems of organizational members, which may be wildly divergent on an individual level, but are emergent in aggregate at the institutional level. These pious opinions may be institutionally nurtured or suppressed, depending upon whether the organization is spiritually enriched or deprived.

Alcoholics Anonymous is both organizationally pious and spiritually enriched, as members create themselves and their organization through their communicative practices. The degree of organizational piety manifested in AA has prompted some researchers to propose that the organization is religious or cult-like (e.g., Cain, 1963; Ellis & Schoenfeld, 1990; Iannaccone, 1992; Rudy & Greil, 1988). In general, however, cults are earmarked by religious or spiritual overtones (Kennedy, 1992; Manuto, 1991; Young & Griffith, 1992), personal vulnerability of its members (Cooper, 1991; Marcus, 1988; Whitsett, 1992; Zerin, 1990), and charismatic leadership (most notoriously Jim Jones and David Koresh). Although Alcoholics Anonymous manifests some cult-like characteristics (e.g., overt spirituality in the organization; leaders' influence; member vulnerability upon entry to the organization), it is not "specifically religious," which Galanter (1990, p. 643) posits is a defining concept for a cult. This begs the question of whether spiritually enriched organizations bring about positive outcomes for themselves and their members.

Organizational Valence

One unintended and sometimes devastating consequence of organizational spirituality occurs when personal spirituality and transcendence are acknowledged at the organizational level, and the nature of the collective spirituality becomes synergistically destructive. This typically occurs through a transformation brought about by charismatic leadership, combined with subjugation of organizational democracy to individual power. Dramatic illustrations of this occurred in Jonestown and Waco. Jim Jones and David Koresh both disembedded organizational features of their religious institutions, transformed them, and reconstituted them at the local level as institutional structures in ways that proved catastrophic for the local organizations. Although both of these groups were overtly religious as well as spiritual (thus meeting Galanter's [1990] criterion for cults), their cases provide vivid exemplars of organizational spirituality, and agent/institution interactions that can result in cataclysmic ends. Thus, spirituality and organizational behaviors may evince a positive or negative *valence.*

Rather than being a valuative term, the concept of valence in this context is drawn from the physical sciences. It refers a cultural ionization or magnetization, in the sense that it attracts or repels. Thus, the valence of an organization may be viewed differently by organizational members than by external observers (e.g., members of a street gang view behaviors that harm others to be rites or rituals that are in keeping with the spirituality of the gang).

In summary, organizations, whether spiritually deprived or spiritually enriched, are constituted of spiritual beings, whose interactions bring to presence an aggregate organizational spirituality. Spirituality need not be acknowledged or denied for it to be manifest in the organization, in whole or in part. This idea engenders new possibilities for research that is grounded in structuration theory and guided by extending conceptions of organizational culture to include organizational spirituality.

Suggestions for Future Research

The concept of organizational spirituality can help address current concerns for organizational survival in an increasingly globalized world. Mahoney, Huff, & Huff (1994) are moving in that direction by positing that "altruism, ethics, goodwill, moral sentiments, and trust need to be placed in the foreground of our [organizational] vision" (p. 153). In a similar vein, Mitroff, Mason, and Pearson (1994) propose five new organizational entities. One of these entities addresses the well-being, development, and recovery of human constituents; a second, called the "World Service/Spiritual Center," focuses on world service and global health. This reconceptualization of organizations recognizes the importance of the personal and global interconnectedness of human agents for organizations to thrive. It is not simply a matter of humanitarianism for its own sake; it is a matter of organizational and global survival. In this regard, the corporate sector may learn much from its spiritually enriched, non-corporate siblings.

Future studies might explore organizational spirituality by focusing on the critical agent/institution/agency interactions from a structurationist perspective. The following five features, in particular, offer guideposts that may indicate spiritually enriched organizations: 1) structures of signification (symbolic action; language) that address synergism or a power greater than the individual members; 2) structures of legitimation (normative action) that encourage altruism, morality, or community; 3) structures of domination (allocation or authorization of resources) that invest organizational resources toward a greater good, even beyond the organization; 4) visionary or charismatic leadership that embodies the "soul" of an organization or its components; and 5) human agents engaged in transcendent or extraordinary action, which can be conceptualized as Eisenberg's (1990) "jamming" or Csikszentmihalyi's "flow" (Csikszentmihalyi, 1975; Csikszentmihalyi & Selega-Csikszentmihalyi, 1989; Csikszentmihalyi, 1990; 1993). These five features can provide an ontological approach to praxis that considers human beings in organizations as more than mere "human resources," and an organizational position of social responsibility in an increasingly global environment as not only an economic or ecological convenience, but a human imperative.

In addition to newly-raised questions concerning organizational spirituality, several questions remain unanswered by this essay, which can be considered only a preliminary investigation. First, the interrelationships between the self and organization bear further research. Occupational scientists recognize that the ways in which people spend time – their occupations – are "always pregnant with meaning. Occupation is a uniquely human enterprise because of the extent of its symbolic vehicle" (Clark, Parham, Carlson, Frank, Jackson, Pierce, Wolfe, & Zemke, 1991, p. 301). A structurationist approach to inquiry can help scholars view the ways in which organization and self are co-constructed.

A second question concerns the nature of charismatic organizations. As indicated earlier, Alcoholics Anonymous has been compared with cults. What, then, is the precise difference between organizations similar to AA and cults, in terms of the communication practices that constitute the organizational culture? There are some clear similarities in the features of each type of organization, including charismatic leadership, ontological shifts in the members, and an emphasis on things spiritual. One difference may be the way in which Alcoholics Anonymous maintains a clear focus on its mission of recovery. What structures prevent spiritually enriched organizations from the engaging in the extreme organizational behaviors that sometimes characterize cults? Finally, future research should address how cult-like organizations might develop safeguards against corruption that leads to destructive collective action.

This essay reconceptualized organizational culture as characterized by organizational spirituality. This knowledge may provide a fuller understanding of the ways in which the self and the institution is co-constructed through everyday lived experience, and help guide future research for organizational survival and human successes in organizations.

References

Albanese, C. L. (1993). Fisher Kings and public places: The old new age in the 1990s. *Annals of the American Academy of Political and Social Science, 527*, 131-143.

Alcoholics Anonymous. (3rd ed.). (1976). New York: Alcoholics Anonymous.

As Bill sees it: The AA way of life (selected writings of AA's co-founder). (1967). New York: Alcoholics Anonymous World Services.

Bateson, G. (1972). *Steps to an ecology of mind.* New York: Ballantine.

Berger, P. & Luckmann, T. (1967). *The social construction of reality.* New York: Doubleday.

Bineham, J. L. (1989). Consensus theory and religious belief. *Communication Studies, 40,* 141-155.

Boozer, R. W. & Maddox, E. N. (1992). An exercise for exploring organizational spirituality: The case of teaching transformational leadership. *Journal of Management Education, 16.* 503-507.

Brandt, E. (1996). Corporate pioneers explore spirituality. *HRMagazine : On Human Resource Management, 41*(4). 82-87.

Brizer, D. A. (1993). Religiosity and drug abuse among psychiatric inpatients. *American Journal of Drug and Alcohol Abuse, 19,* 337-345.

Burke, K. (1954). *Permanence and change.* (Rev. Ed.). Los Altos, CA: Hermes.

Cain, A. H. (1963, February). Alcoholics Anonymous: Cult or cure? *Harper's magazine,* 48-52.

Carroll, S. (1993). Spirituality and purpose in life in alcoholism recovery. *Journal of Studies on Alcohol, 54,* 297-301.

Cooley, F. B. & Lasser, D. (1992). Managing alcohol abuse in a family context. *American Family Physician, 45,* 1735-1739.

Cooper, P. S. (1991). *The relationship between adolescent self-concept and interest in cults.* M.A. Thesis, University of Houston.

Csikszentmihalyi, M. (1975). *Beyond boredom and anxiety.* San Francisco: Jossey-Bass.

Csikszentmihalyi, M. (1990). *Flow: The psychology of optimal experience.* New York: Harper & Row.

Csikszentmihalyi, M. (1993). *The evolving self: A psychology for the third millennium.* New York: HarperCollins.

Csikszentmihalyi, M. & Selega-Csikszentmihalyi, I. (Eds.). (1989). *Optimal experience: Psychological studies of flow in consciousness.* New York: Cambridge University Press.

Dehler, G. E. & Welsh, M. A. (1994). Spirituality and organizational transformation: Implications for the new management program. *Journal of Managerial Psychology, 9,* 17-26

Denzin, N. K. (1987a). *The alcoholic self.* Newbury Park, CA: Sage.

Denzin, N. K. (1987b). *The recovering alcoholic.* Newbury Park, CA: Sage.

Denzin, N. K. (1988). The alcoholic self: Communication, ritual, and identity transformation. In D. R. Maines & C. J. Couch (Eds.), *Communication and social structure* Springfield, IL: Charles C. Thomas.

Diaz, V., Caplan, A., & Mauer, S. M. (1993). A transplant of real life. *Pediatric Nephrology, 7,* 585-588.

Eisenberg, E. (1990). Jamming: Transcendence through organizing. *Communication Research, 17,* 139-164.

Ellis, A. & Schoenfeld, E. (1990). Divine intervention and the treatment of chemical dependency. *Journal of Substance Abuse, 2,* 459-468.

Fox, M. (1994). *The reinvention of work: A new vision of livelihood for our time.* New York: HarperCollins.

Frohock, F. M. (1993). *Healing powers: Alternative medicine, spiritual communities, and the state,* Chicago: University of Chicago Press.

Galanter, M. (1990). Cults and zealous self-help movements: A psychiatric perspective. *The American Journal of Psychiatry, 147,* 543-551.

Geertz, C. (1973). *The interpretation of cultures.* New York: Basic.

Gelman, D. Leonard, E. A., & Fisher, B. (1991). Clean and sober – and agnostic: Turned off by AA's religious aspects, new groups are leaving God out of the battle with the bottle. *Newsweek, 118,* 62-63.

Giddens, A. (1976). *New rules of sociological method: A positive critique of interpretative sociologies.* New York: Basic.

Giddens, A. (1979). *Central problems in social theory: Action, structure and contradiction in social analysis.* Berkeley, CA: University of California Press.

Giddens, A. (1981). *A contemporary critique of historical materialism.* Berkeley, CA: University of California Press.

Giddens, A. (1984). *The constitution of society: Outline of the theory of structuration.* Berkeley, CA: University of California Press.

Goodall, H. L., Jr. (1993). Mysteries of the future told: Communication as the material manifestation of spirituality. *World Communication Journal, 22,* 40-49.

Hanna, F. J. (1992). Reframing spirituality: AA, the 12 steps, and the mental health counselor. *Journal of Mental Health Counseling, 14,* 166-179.

Hawley, J. (1993). *Reawakening the spirit in work: The power of Dharmic management.* San Francisco: Berrett-Koehler.

Heise, R. G. (1991). *Spirituality and contented sobriety: A model.* Ed.D. Dissertation, Memphis State University.

Heise, R. G., & Steitz, J. A. (1991). Religious perfectionism versus spiritual growth. *Counseling and Values, 36,* 11-18.

Hikins, J. W. (1989). Through the rhetorical looking-glass: Consensus theory and fairy tales in the epistemology of communication – a reply to Bineham. *Communication Studies, 40,* 161-171.

Iannaccone, L. R. (1992). Sacrifice and stigma: Reducing free-riding in cults, communes, and other collectives. *Journal of Political Economy, 100,* 271-291.

Jones, C., Wainwright, G., & Yarnold, E. (Eds.). (1986) *The study of spirituality.* New York: Oxford University Press.

Kaufman, E. (1990-91). Critical aspects of the psychodynamics of substance abuse and the evaluation of their application to a psychotherapeutic approach. *International Journal of the Additions, 25,* 97-114.

Kennedy, S. T. (1992). *Boundary management and self-differentiation: A comparison of members in a cult/new religious movement with groups or students.* Ph.D. Dissertation, Boston University.

Kirkwood, W. G. (1994). Studying communication about spirituality and the spiritual consequences of communication. *The Journal of Communication and Religion, 17*(1), 13-26. [*Online*] Available: http://www.cios.org/www/jcr/jcr-v17n1.html

Madhere, S. (1993). Acceptance, resistance, and the value system of young adults. *Psychological Reports, 73,* 1403-1406.

Mahoney, J. T., Huff, A. S., & Huff, J. O. (1994). Toward a new social contract theory in organization science. *Journal of Management Inquiry, 3,* 153-168.

Manuto, R. J. (1991). *"Brainwashing": Cults and the first amendment.* Ph.D. Dissertation, University of Oregon.

Marcus, C. S. (1988). *Assessing adolescent vulnerability to cult affiliation.* Ph.D. Dissertation, Yeshiva University.

McGuire, M. B. (1993). Health and spirituality as contemporary concerns. *Annals of the American Academy of Political and Social Science, 527,* 144-154.

McKee, D. D. & Chappel, J. N. (1992). Spirituality and medical practice. *Journal of Family Practice, 35*, 201-207.

Meyerson, D. E. (1991). "Normal" ambiguity? A glimpse of an occupational culture. In P. J. Frost, L. F. Moore, C. C. Lundberg, & J. Martin (Eds.). *Reframing organizational culture* (pp. 131-144). Newbury Park, CA: Sage.

Mitroff, I., Mason, R. O., & Pearson, C. M. (1994). Radical surgery: What will tomorrow's organizations look like? *Academy of Management Executive, 8,* 11-21.

Morgan, P. P. & Cohen, L. (1994). Spirituality slowly gaining recognition among North American psychiatrists. *Canadian Medical Association Journal, 150,* 582-585.

Mumby, D. K., & Putnam, L. L. (1992). The politics of emotion: A feminist reading of bounded rationality. *Academy of Management Review, 17.* 465-486.

Neck, C. P. & Milliman, J. F. (1994). Thought self-leadership: Finding spiritual fulfillment in organizational life. *Journal of Managerial Psychology, 9,* 9-16.

Palermo, G. B., Simpson, D., Knudten, R., Turci, V., & Davis, H. (1993). Modes of defensive behavior in a violent society. *International Journal of Offender Therapy and Comparative Criminology, 37,* 251-261.

Pokora, R. (1996). *And Mary danced: Communication and spirituality at a women's religious organization.* Unpublished doctoral dissertation, Purdue University, West Lafayette, IN.

Prasinos, S. (1992). Spiritual aspects of psychotherapy. *Journal of Religion and Health, 31,* 41-52.

Prezioso, F. A. (1986). Spirituality and the treatment of substance abuse. ERIC Document ED 278916.

Pringle, R. (1989). Bureaucracy, rationality, and sexuality: The case of secretaries. In J. Hearn, D. L. Sheppard, P. Tancred-Sheriff, & G. Burell (Eds.). *The sexuality of organizations* (pp. 158-177). London: Sage.

Pym, A. (1997). Beyond postmodernity: Grounding ethics in spirit. *Electronic Journal of Communication. 7*(1). [*Online.*] Available: http://www.cios.org/getfile\PYM_V7N197

Reed, P. G. (1993). An emerging paradigm for the investigation of spirituality in nursing. *Research in Nursing & Health, 15,* 349-357.

Resnick, M. D., Harris, L. J., & Blum, R. W. (1993). The impact of caring and connectedness on adolescent health and well-being. *Journal of Paediatrics and Child Health, 29,* S3-S9.

Riley, P. (1983). A structurationist account of political culture.

Administrative Science Quarterly, 28, 414-437.

Roof, W. C. (1993). Toward the year 2000: Reconstructions of religious space. *Annals of the American Academy of Political and Social Science, 527,* 155-170.

Rudy, D. R., & Greil, A. L. (1988). Is Alcoholics Anonymous a religious organization:? Meditations on marginality. *Sociological Analysis, 50,* 41-51.

Schmidt, R. M. (1993). Health Watch: Health promotion and disease prevention in primary care. *Methods of Information in Medicine, 32,* 245-248.

Schneider, K. J. (1993). Hitchcock's Vertigo: An existential view of spirituality. *Journal of Humanistic Psychology, 33,* 91-100.

Scott, R. L. (1989). Rhetoric and spirituality: Three issues – a reply to Bineham. *Communication Studies, 40,* 172-176.

Sheridan, M. J., Bullis, R. K., Adcock, C. R., Berlin, S. D., & Miller, P. C. (1992). Practitioners personal and professional attitudes and behaviors toward religion and spirituality: Issues for education and practice. *Journal of Social Work Education, 28,* 190-203.

Smith, C. R. (1993). The problem with writing on rhetorical charisma, power, and spirituality. *The Journal of Communication and Religion. 16*(2), 83-97. [*Online.*] Available: http://www.cios.org/www/jcr/jcr-v16n2.html

Stafford, T. (1991). The hidden gospel of the 12 steps: Understanding the origins of the recovery movement can help Christians know how to relate to it today. *Christianity Today, 35,* 14-19.

Strauss, A. (1959). *Mirrors and masks: The search for identity.* New York: Free Press.

Stein, B. (1988). Hollywood: God is nigh. *Newsweek, 112,* 8.

Thune, C. E. (1977). Alcoholism and the archetypical past: A phenomenological perspective on Alcoholics Anonymous. *Quarterly Journal of Studies on Alcohol, 38,* 75-88.

Travasino, R. (1981). Alternation and conversion as qualitatively different transformations. In G. P. Stone & H. A. Farberman, (Eds.), *Social Psychology through Symbolic Interaction.* (pp. 237-248), New York: Wiley.

Tukey, D. D. (1989). What's at stake? A reply to Bineham. *Communication Studies, 40,*156-160.

Tukey, David D. (1995). Researching "ultimate" communication: A response to Kirkwood and a research agenda. *The Journal of Communication and Religion. 18*(2), 65-72.

Twelve steps and twelve traditions. (1953).New York: Alcoholics Anonymous World Services.

Uva, J. L. (1991). Alcoholics Anonymous: Medical recovery through a higher power. *Journal of the American Medical Association, 266,* 3065-3067.

Valentine, L. & Feinauer, L. L. (1993). Resilience factors associated with female survivors of childhood sexual abuse. *American Journal of Family Therapy, 21,* 216-224.

Vaughan, F. (1991). Spiritual issues in psychotherapy. *Journal of Transpersonal Psychology, 23,* 105-119.

Waldram, J. B. (1993). Aboriginal spirituality: Symbolic healing in Canadian prisons. *Culture Medicine and Psychiatry, 17,* 345-362.

Wallace, J. (1982). Alcoholism from the inside out: A phenomenological analysis. In N.J. Estes & M. E. Heinemann, (Eds.). *Alcoholism: Development, consequences, and interventions.* (pp. 1-23). St. Louis, MO: Mosby.

Watts, R. J. (1993). Community action through manhood development: A look at concepts and concerns from the frontline. *American Journal of Community Psychology, 21,* 333-359.

Weaver, R. L. & Cotrell, H. W. (1992). A nonreligious spirituality that causes students to clarify their values and to respond with passion. *Education, 112,* 426-435.

Whitsett, D. P. (1992). A self psychological approach to the cult phenomenon. *Clinical Social Work Journal, 20,* 363-375.

Witmer, D. F. (1997). Communication and recovery: Structuration as an ontological approach to organizational culture. *Communication Monographs, 64,* 324-349.

Witmer, J. M. & Sweeney, T. J. (1992). A holistic model for wellness and prevention over the life span. *Journal of Counseling and Development, 71,* 140-148.

Young, J. L., & Griffith, E. E. H. (1992). A critical evaluation of coercive persuasion as used in the assessment of cults. *Behavioral Sciences & the Law, 10,* 89-101.

Zerin, M. B. F. (1990). *The Pied Piper phenomenon: Family systems and vulnerability to cults.* Ph.D. Dissertation, The Fielding Institute.

Zimmerman, M. A. & Maton, K. I. (1992). Life style and substance use among male African-American urban adolescents: A cluster analytic approach. *American Journal of Community Psychology, 20,* 121-138.

Chapter 2

Reframing Organizational Communication Theory and Research Through Spirituality

Kathy Krone
University of Nebraska-Lincoln

Abstract

Different constructs and processes in organizational communication theory can be enhanced by investigating their spiritual underpinnings and potential. In this paper I begin such a project by broadening the notion of work to include "inner work" and discussing its relationship to the construction of work that is "good." Understanding the significance of maintaining a continuous relationship between inner work and outer work enlarges the domain of organizational communication research and leads to the reconceptualization of several traditional organizational communication processes. In this paper I discuss the need for investigations of inner work and its relationship to outer work, and research on the role of message production, re-framing, and leader-member relationships in the production of good work.

21

> *"The breeze is the merest puff, but you yourself sail headlong and*
> *breathless under the gale force of spirit."*
> *(Annie Dillard, 1988, p. 13)*

The past decade has witnessed an explosion of popular books on the power of spirituality in the workplace. The authors of these books reframe leadership as stewardship (Block, 1996), work as "sacred" (Fox, 1994), and rely on the language of spirituality to offer advice on enhancing managerial effectiveness (Jones, 1995; Klein & Izzo, 1998), reducing stress, and increasing personal and organizational productivity (Jones, 1995; Klein & Izzo, 1998; Orsborn, 1992) (see also Nadesan, 1999, for additional examples). The continued commercial popularity of this literature as we enter the 21st century, suggests that the human need to integrate spirituality and work is something other than a passing fad.

Certainly, organizations and contemporary work arrangements have the capacity to deaden the liveliest of spirits, leaving us questioning whether and how our work can be made more meaningful. Chronic, budgetary belt-tightening, relentless pressure to do more with less, sudden reorganizations and downsizing can leave us feeling disoriented, lifeless and dispirited. Even a host of human resource programs purportedly designed to empower, enliven and emotionally engage employees, are just as likely to tighten the reins of organizational control (Argyris, 1998; Barker, 1993; Sennett, 1998). Driven nearly exclusively by economic rationality, all large organizations, even well-intentioned ones, have the capacity to inflict great spiritual harm.

While few organizations appear to take seriously their spirit-crushing capacities, increasingly they are beginning to acknowledge the presence of some sort of spiritual impulse and its potential to enhance organizational effectiveness. Spirituality has been credited for helping employees find meaning in their work and for helping them regain stability during times of organizational change and upheaval (Lincoln Journal Star, 9/5/2000). Some organizations have even set aside "karma rooms" or "meditation rooms" in which individual employees privately pray, reflect, or calm themselves (Laabs, 1995). Profit-driven organizations may reduce spirituality to one more human resource to be managed. Harnessing or taming spirit in this way risks converting the experience and expression of spirituality to a form of spiritual labor (Fineman, 2000). To date, few authors of popular books and articles envision autonomous expressions of spirituality that might question and challenge harmful organizational practices.

For the most part, we in communication studies lag behind organizational practitioners in publicly acknowledging the importance of human spirituality. While we are less likely than management consultants to approach spirituality as a source of economic advantage, we also, though, have been reluctant to recognize spirit as a fundamental life force and source of human energy in our theorizing and research. The purpose of this paper is to begin to reclaim a role for spirit in organizational communication theorizing and research. In order to do so, I first rely on spirituality to expand the notion of work to include inner work. I then discuss the importance of cultivating a relationship between spiritually-minded inner work and the work we do in the public sphere. Last, I discuss how maintaining a continuous relationship between inner work and outer work enlarges the domain of organizational communication research and can lead to the reframing of several prominent organizational communication theories.

Spirituality, Inner Work and Good Work

"We wake, if we wake at all, to mystery ..."
(Annie Dillard, 1988, p. 13)

Understandings of spirituality and of what it means to be spiritual are somewhat contested (Chittister, 1998). As the above quote suggests though, to be spiritually awake is to struggle with potentially unanswerable questions related to why we are here, how we should live, and what our place is in the universe (Ganje-Fling & McCarthy, 1996). Spirituality is a broad construct and should not be confused with the narrower construct of religion (Wong, 1998). While religion is meant to nourish human spirituality, it is not the same thing as being spiritual (Dalai Lama & Cutler, 1998). Spirituality has been conceived of as inner transformation achieved through a process of mental development (Dalai Lama & Cutler, 1998), as a quest for meaning, as self-transcendence, or as taking a heroic stance in the face of suffering (Frankl, 1969). It also has been understood as a process of becoming more fully alive (Fox, 1991). Turning toward understanding spirituality as a form of intelligence, some even view constructing the laws of physics as a spiritual process since Stephen Hawking, the brilliant theoretical physicist, has claimed God is to be found there. Spirituality as a form of intelligence also echoes throughout the work of those who claim spirituality is grounded in unitive thinking, a particular type of cognitive processing ability that animates human creativity, intuition, and insightfulness, and therefore, helps us live more meaningful lives (Zohar & Marshall, 2000).

While there are many frameworks with which to understand spirituality, in this paper I rely on the creation spirituality tradition for guidance for at least two reasons. First, creation spirituality is rooted in a blend of both Eastern and Western thought, and, as such, is much more inclusive than most spiritual traditions. Second, since this tradition views spirit simply as a life force, as breath, and as energy, everyone has access to it.

Creation spirituality has been characterized as a liberation theology for "first world" peoples who must struggle to reclaim their under-developed spirits from over-developed economies (Fox, 1991). As a theology of struggle, creation spirituality is rooted in the understanding that the spiritual is also political (Boff, 1989). While spirituality tends to be downplayed in traditional theological thought and religious practice, it is of great importance to liberation theology (Boff, 1984; 1989; Gutierrez, 1988). The human spirit is made dull by powerful economic and political systems that assure material comfort, but seem unable to bring deeper meaning or lasting happiness to our lives (Lane, 2000). Inner work is required to recover our suppressed spiritual experience from these systems. Creation spirituality can usefully guide this inner work by animating the collective experience of indignation in response to oppression, and inspiring resistance to deadening work and social arrangements (Fox, 1991). It also energizes the capacity to imagine and construct more life-sustaining forms of work (Fox, 1994).

Creation spirituality conceptualizes life as a spiritual journey consisting of four interwoven paths. Separately and together, these paths remind us of what is important and of how we can expect to experience a "divine presence" in our lives (Fox, 1983). The first of these, the *via negativa*, instructs us to the meaning of pain, suffering, and loss in our lives and of the need to accept nothingness, to be silent and to let go. The *via positiva* calls our attention to the significance of experiencing awe and wonder in the process of encountering the mysteries of nature and the universe. The *via creativa* reminds us of our own capacities to create beauty and to understand this process as one of co-creation with the divine. Finally, the *via transformativa* instructs us to the importance of taking action to relieve suffering and to combat injustice (Fox, 1983).

Underlying these four paths is an on-going tension between the need for mysticism (i.e., a holding still), and the need for prophecy (i.e., action). Through the practice of holding still, we tap into a universal life force and begin to regain the capacity to wonder and create, capacities that too often have been dulled through organizational experience. Through prophecy we are called to speak out and to act against systems of injustice. Holding still and calling for change are interdependent processes. In order to speak out effectively against injustice, prophesizing must be guided by what has been learned during periods of inaction. Periods of silence and inaction are necessary in order to reflect upon and learn from action taken against injustice. Balancing the on-going tension between holding still and calling for change is a route toward revitalizing our spirits, knowing ourselves deeply, and living out who we are in the world (Fox, 1991; 1994).

The practice of holding still is akin to various practices associated with inner work. Inner work does not have to be spiritual, however, a-spiritual inner work is more likely to perpetuate harmful forms of outer work in the world. Inner work, devoid of spirituality, easily becomes ego-driven, and as such, also is more likely to fuel an egocentric approach to work. Focusing exclusively on work as a source of personal gratification provides little incentive to discern meaningless from meaningful forms of work, or to examine the ways in which our work may bring harm to others. As spirituality deepens, so does the awareness of the possibility of something more important than individual success at work. Through spiritually-minded inner work, we can learn to see the extent to which we have internalized an organizational "eye" and begin to turn away from the habit of seeing ourselves as the organization sees us, and judging ourselves exclusively according to its standards and values. Through the discipline of spiritually-minded inner work, we begin to reclaim and articulate those dimensions of our spiritual experience that have been systematically suppressed. Through an on-going interplay between spiritual inner work and acting to question or aggressively challenge organizational injustices, we continue to develop the capacity to discern meaningless or harmful work from that which is good, and re-kindle a desire to express ourselves through "good work".

Inner work then, should cultivate spiritual development, strengthening the resolve and capacity to make work good. Work becomes good when it provides necessary and useful products/services, enables us to use our unique talents and gifts, and is done cooperatively with others, thereby freeing us from egocentricity (Schumacher, 1979). Good work is spiritually meaningful in that it connects us to unseen forces much larger than our individual needs and desires (Fox, 1994). Inner work that is spiritual motivates the transformation of traditional work in to work that is good. Educational organizations can be transformed from "knowledge factories" into "wisdom schools", the practice of medicine can become more holistic, and businesses can become more socially responsive, responsible and environmentally sensitive (Fox, 1994). Acknowledging the importance of a spiritual dimension to inner work, and the importance of spiritual development to the formation of work that is good enlarges the organizational communication research agenda and leads to the re-conceptualization of traditional organizational communication processes. In the following section I discuss four possibilities: (a) investigations of inner work as it relates to outer work and the increasing pull toward doing good work; (b) research on message production in the service of good work, (c) research on re-framing and its relationship to good work, and (d) research on the formation of leader-member relationships and their role in the production of good work.

Inner Work, Good Work, and Organizational Communication Research

> *"...when work is soulless, life stifles and dies."*
> *(Albert Camus, cited in Schumacher, 1979)*

Organizational communication research focuses almost exclusively on those forms of work for which people are paid. The nature of the inner work that people do, and the ways in which their inner and outer work inform each other, have yet to be taken seriously as a focus of research. Though unpaid, the various ways in which people reflect upon and learn from their work experience constitutes a legitimate form of work that warrants further exploration. In particular, organizational communication studies could examine ways in which inner work frees and fails to free us from participating in systematically oppressive work arrangements.

For example, remembering and reflecting on dreams about work is a form of inner work that can be particularly interdependent with spiritual development and the enhanced capacity to reflect critically upon the ways in which we have internalized external constraints. Since without any effort, our dreams are creative (Lukeman, 1990; Neu, 1980), recalling and working with our dreams re-connects us with the inborn capacity to be creative. In addition, characterized by some as a way to listen to God (Kelsey, 1978), dreams can offer insights regarding unsettling situations at work that effectively penetrate local ideology. Reflecting on dream imagery and what it communicates about who we are in relationship with our work, then, is a way to explore and begin to appreciate our deepest mysteries. Because dreams reveal the complexity and artistry of our inner being (Lukeman, 1990; Neu, 1980), remembering them and working with them can revitalize our creative capacities which may have been systematically dulled. Remembering and working with dreams also can strengthen us to be faithful to how we interpret our own experience, enabling us to exercise greater interpretive control at work. Used in this way, dream work has the potential to gradually change our lives and our orientation to work.

Studies of dream imagery and interpretation are a way to access the meaning of work experience and its place in the dreamer's waking life. It also is a way to better understand and contribute to the dreamers' on-going development and relationship to their work. Carefully conducted, such studies could simultaneously contribute to the recovery and articulation of experience that has been systematically suppressed because it, in some way, might have threatened dominant group members or even presented the dreamers themselves with insights they might not yet have been ready to face.

For instance, in my own experience, a recent dream reminded me that "the good life is within you". This dream occurred some months following a rather conflicted decision I had made to remain living and working in the state of Nebraska. If you have entered Nebraska via any of the major highways, you may remember having been greeted by a sign that announces: "Nebraska – The good life." When I awoke with the above message echoing in my consciousness, I felt somehow assured that something about what makes life good comes from within us, rather than exclusively from the geographical space we happen to occupy at any point in time. Dreams such as this might be considered generative in that they produce new insights and understandings that make an important difference in how the dreamer might then relate to a previously unsettling situation or experience. The scope of organizational communication study can be usefully broadened and deepened by including this, and other forms of inner work, as legitimate foci for research.

Message Production in the Service of Good Work

Having acknowledged the existence of a spiritual impulse, and the relationship between spiritual development and the desire to pursue good work, we then are challenged to reconsider traditional conceptualizations of message production and approaches to interpersonal influence in organizations. Many noteworthy advances have been made in message production theorizing in recent years (see, for example, Burleson & Planalp, 2000; D. O'Keefe, 1994; Waldron, 1997; Wilson, 1997). However, taking spirituality and the possibility of spiritual development seriously would lead to a more radical re-conceptualization of message production processes. In particular, we might re-consider the ways in which we traditionally understand message source and message effectiveness.

Infusing message production theorizing with spirituality reminds us that important and useful messages can originate from places other than the individual intellect. For example, in her description of Quaker meeting practices, Louis (1994) offers a spiritual way in which to understand message production. In the Quaker tradition, the source of what is said during meetings lies beyond the individual.   In silence, meeting participants hold still in order to discern guidance from a much larger force. Messages grow as communicants wait, together, in silence. As messages grow and a member becomes ready to speak, message simplicity is favored over rhetorical finesse. Dramatic, embellished messages, or prepared speeches that would draw attention to the individual are discouraged in favor of simple messages articulated with humility (Louis, 1994). The Quaker practice of combining speech with holding still, is akin to the entwined practices of inaction and action called for within the creation spirituality tradition. Through spiritual experience, we tap in to a force much larger than our individual selves. This transcendent force can be understood as a source of messages and message growth.

Traditional conceptualizations of message production tend to emphasize its instrumental, goal-oriented nature, and its usefulness in managing the activities of others. Cognitively sophisticated messages (B. O' Keefe, 1990) as well as strategically ambiguous ones (Eisenberg, 1984) are theorized as being more effective in coordinating and regulating others' behavior, at least when produced by management. When produced by more marginalized organizational members, it is not at all clear that either approach is likely to be effective (see for example, Bingham & Burleson, 1989).   By infusing message production theorizing with spirituality, and by assuming that spiritually awake individuals are more likely to challenge injustice or question decisions rooted in purely instrumental reasoning, we might need to reconsider what message effectiveness means.

Cultivating spirituality through inner work clarifies the values necessary to pursue good work and increases the likelihood of challenging practices that perpetuate harmful treatment of others and harmful work. Because harmful systems of work may be relatively closed and resistant to change, any single protest message, no matter how rhetorically sophisticated or strategically ambiguous, is unlikely to effect change. Still, a slightly veiled threat expressing an awareness of one's legal rights, or the

pointed use of humor (see, for example, Brown, 1993) ma
and provoke a moment of self-reflection among those who
Responding in the moment, in these ways, signals a refusal to simply let a
harmful act pass. When used by victims, these types of messages might
constitute a kind of "strategic ambiguity for the oppressed." While
stopping short of rationally engaging an argument that most likely cannot
be won, these messages can play an important role in the on-going struggle
for interpretive control over the human beings we are becoming through
our work. Responding in the moment, even if simply to label a harmful
situation as such, contributes to our spiritual development. Messages of
this sort are unlikely to awaken or change a fundamentally oppressive
system. At best, they might introduce discontinuity into otherwise closed
systems, momentarily disrupting the otherwise seamless flow of
instrumental interaction. The enduring impact of these messages in
controlling others or in changing the larger system, however, is not the
important point. From a spiritual point of view, their greatest value may
lie simply in articulating them at all and in so doing, reminding ourselves
of who we are and of what is of greatest importance.

In sum, message production theorizing can be both broadened and
deepened by considering the role of spiritual development in message
production. Taking spirituality seriously will require considering
alternatives to human sources of messages and re-considering the meaning
of message effectiveness.

Re-framing and Good Work

Organizational communication studies can be enriched by
acknowledging the role of some sort of spiritual impulse in creative re-
framing, especially in response to oppressive circumstances. Spirituality
animates creativity and is associated with the capacity to depart from
convention (Zohar & Marshall, 2000), both of which can be useful in
negotiating organizational constraints. Developing spirituality through
inner work can nourish and fuel what Sally Gearhart (1982) calls
"resourcement." Resourcement refers to the process of disengaging from a
system enough to think critically about it, while also remaining engaged
with it enough to speak and act creatively within it. Through
resourcement, organizational members develop radically creative
responses that frame an issue differently.

Organizational communication studies can be enhanced by locating
and describing instances of resourcement simply to learn more about what
inspires and guides these creative accomplishments. Understanding the

dynamics of resourcement also might be useful in instructing others on its possibilities for creating space in which to express alternative values within systems of constraint.   I witnessed an inspiring example of resourcement while collecting data in a large manufacturing organization which had, at the time, recently decided to implement a series of programs requiring greater involvement and cooperation between labor and management leaders.

As a part of this change, monthly public meetings were being held in which union leaders and managers came together to reveal budgetary information and discuss how each business unit was contributing to the health and viability of the overall operation. I observed three different supervisors publicly reporting on the status of their respective business units. Each business unit supervisor was required to provide the larger audience with information on absenteeism, financial losses due to the production of scrap, and OSHA recordable injuries.   While each supervisor dutifully reported the data required in each of these areas, one of these enlivened his presentation by going on to reframe absenteeism as something called "presenteeism" in which he then publicly recognized two of his employees for not having missed a day of work in 17 years. After reporting on the amount of scrap produced by his unit, he went on to publicly recognize the work group that had produced the least amount of scrap as "The Scrapbusters."   Similarly, after reporting the number of injuries incurred by employees in his unit, he went on to recognize with the "Golden Broom Award" the work group that had kept their unit most clean, thereby reducing the likelihood of injury.

While I have no way of knowing whether this business unit manager considers himself spiritual in any of the senses described earlier, he clearly was able to not only accommodate the rather negative organizational mandate to publicly report on the various ways in which his unit had fallen short over a given time period, but also to creatively reframe those reports in a spirited way. In stepping beyond the conventional and rather lifeless reporting format, he created space in which to express the unique spirit of his business unit and his own values as a manager.   The scope of organizational communication studies might be similarly enlivened by attending to the tenacity, courage and creativity required to provide leadership in ways that express spiritual values while also accommodating corporate values.

Leader-Member Relationships and Good Work

Theories of leader-member relationships also can be re-framed through spirituality. Spiritually-minded studies would be interested in learning more about the relational context of work and ways in which webs of leader-member relationships support and undermine the pursuit of good work. Since the practice of good work requires cooperation with others (Schumacher, 1979), it is difficult to imagine good work emerging from a system of "bad" relationships. Bad relationships in this sense, would be those cultivating egocentricity rather than qualities that would be more likely to foster self-transcendence. Since self-transcendence is more likely to occur while working collaboratively, organizational communication studies could do more to acknowledge the importance of collaborative leader-member relationships to the pursuit of good work. Spiritually-minded studies of leader-member relationships, then, would be interested in learning more about how the power differences inherent to them, shape communication patterns that fuel egocentricity rather than self-transcendence via collaboration.

A related and promising avenue of research would be to explore the production of aesthetic moments in leader-member relationships. While all relationships have both instrumental and aesthetic dimensions (Dewey, 1934), ego-centric and collaborative leader-member relationships might produce different moments of ugliness and beauty. For instance, while leader-member relationships serve an instrumental purpose in the routine production of work, they also can be sites of struggle for group members who may be marginalized by their spiritual values and desire for good work. As was discussed earlier, spiritually-minded inner work plays a role in the recovery and articulation of suppressed experience. As this happens, marginalized group members are more likely to experience greater comfort challenging harmful treatment (Hartsock, 1983; 1998). Out of their mutual engagement in struggle, leaders and members may create understandings that neither would have been able to construct alone. Organizational communication studies might examine these experiences for any resemblance they may bear to aesthetic moments.

Conclusion

The purpose of this paper was to begin to identify a role for spirituality in organizational communication theory and research. The increasing human need for meaningful work and meaningful relationships (Spretnak, 1991), and the increasing corporate need to compete aggressively in order to survive, combine to make individuals vulnerable to organizational programs designed to appropriate and manage human spirituality for economic gain. Organizational communication studies can play an important role in questioning organizational attempts to manage and commodify the human spirit. We can do so by focusing our energies on those instances in which spirituality contributes to the ability to recognize, challenge, negotiate and occasionally overcome organizational constraints as well as our own inner constraints that prevent us from learning about the ways in which we have been harmed, or might have also harmed others through our work. Broadening the scope of organizational communication studies to include inner work and communicative processes associated with seeking "good work", presents us with one promising approach. More fundamentally, re-framing organizational communication theory through spirituality humanizes our research agenda, and lays the groundwork for transforming organizational communication research, itself, into work that is good.

References

Argyris, C. (1998). Empowerment: The emperor's new clothes. *Harvard Business Review, May-June,* 98-107.

Barker, J. (1993). Tightening the iron cage: Concertive control in the self-managing organization. *Administrative Science Quarterly, 38,* 408-437.

Bingham, S., & Burleson, B. (1989). Multiple effects of messages with multiple goals: Some perceived outcomes of responses to sexual harassment. *Human Communication Research, 16,* 184-215.

Block, P. (1996). *Stewardship: Choosing service over self-interest.* San Francisco: Berrett-Koehler Publishers.

Boff, L. (1984). *Church, charism, and power: Toward a militant ecclesiology.* New York: Crossroad.

Boff, L. (1989). *When theology listens to the poor.* New York: HarperCollins.

Brown, M. H. (1993). Sex and the workplace: Watch your behind, or they'll watch it for you. In G. L. Kreps (Ed.), *Sexual harassment: Communication implications* (pp. 118-130). Cresskill, NJ: Hampton Press.

Burleson, B. R., & Planalp, S. (2000). Producing emotion(al) messages. *Communication Theory, 10,* 221-250.

Chittister, J. D. (1998). *Heart of flesh: A feminist spirituality for women and men.* Grand Rapids, MI: William B. Eerdmans Publishing Company.

Dalai Lama & Cutler, H. C. (1998). *The art of happiness: A handbook for living.* New York: Riverhead Books.

Dewey, J. (1934). *Art as experience.* New York: Minton, Balch & Company.

Dillard, A. (1988). *Pilgrim at Tinker Creek.* New York: HarperPerennial.

Eisenberg, E. (1984). Ambiguity as strategy in organizational comunication. *Communication Monographs, 51,* 227-242.

Fairhurst, G.T., & Sarr, R.A. (1996). *The art of framing.* San Francisco: Jossey-Bass.

Fineman, S. (2000). Commodifying the emotionally intelligent. In S. Fineman (Ed.), *Emotion in organizations* (pp. 101-114). London: Sage.

Fox, M. (1983). *Original blessing: A primer in creation spirituality.* Santa Fe, NM: Bear & Company.

Fox, M. (1991). *Creation spirituality: Liberating gifts for the peoples of the earth.* New York: HarperCollins Publishers.

Fox, M. (1994). *The reinvention of work: A new vision of livelihood for our time.* New York: HarperCollins Publishers.

Frankl, V. E. (1969). *The will to meaning.* New York: New American Library.

Ganje-Fling, M. A., & McCarthy, P. (1996). Impact of child sexual abuse on client spiritual development: Counseling implications. *Journal of Counseling and Development, 74,* 253-258.

Gearhart, S. (1982). Womanpower: Energy re-sourcement. In C. Spretnak (Ed.), *The politics of women's spirituality: Essays on the rise of spiritual power within the feminist movement* (pp, 194-206). Garden City, NY: Anchor.

Gutierrez, G. (1988). *A theology of liberation.* New York: Orbis Books.

Hartsock, N. C. M. (1983). The feminist standpoint: Developing the ground for a specifically feminist historical materialism. In S. Harding & M. Hintikka (Eds.), *Discovering reality* (pp. 283-310). Boston: Reidel.

Hartsock, N. C. M. (1998). *The feminist standpoint revisited and other essays.* Boulder, CO: Westview Press.

Jones, L. B. (1995). *Jesus CEO.* New York: Hyperion.

Kelsey, M. (1978). *Dreams: A way to listen to God.* New York: Paulist Press.

Klein, E., & Izzo, J. B. (1998). *Awakening corporate soul: Four paths to unleash the power of people at work.* Lion's Bay, BC: Fairwinds Press.

Laabs, J. J. (1995). Balancing spirituality and work. *Personnel Journal, 74,* 60-62.

Lane, R. E. (2000). *The loss of happiness in market democracies.* New Haven: Yale University Press.

Louis, M.R. (1994). In the manner of Friends: Learnings from Quaker practice for organizational renewal. *Journal of Organizational Change Management, 7,* 42-60.

Lukeman, A. (1990). *What your dreams can teach you.* St. Paul, MN: Llewellyn Publications.

Nadesan, M. H. (1999). The discourses of corporate spiritualism and evangelical capitalism. *Management Communication Quarterly, 13,* 3-42.

Neu, E.R. (1988). *Dreams and dream groups: Messages from the interior.* Freedom, CA: The Crossing Press.

O'Keefe, B. J. (1990). The logic of regulative communication: Understanding the rationality of message designs. In J. P. Dillard (Ed.), *Seeking compliance: The production of interpersonal influence messages* (pp. 87-104). Scottsdale, AZ: Gorsuch Scarisbrick.

O'Keefe, D. J. (1994). Compliance gaining: From strategy-based to feature-based analyses of compliance gaining message classification and production. *Communication Theory, 4,* 61-69.

Orsborn, C. M. (1992). *Inner excellence at work: The path to meaning, spirit, and success.* New York: AMACOM.

Schumacher, E. F. (1979). *Good work.* New York: Harper & Row, Publishers.

Sennett, R. (1998). *The corrosion of character: The personal consequences of work in the new capitalism.* New York: Norton.

Spretnak, C. (1991). *States of grace: The recovery of meaning in the postmodern age.* New York: HarperSanFrancisco.

Waldron, V. R. (1997). Toward a theory of interactive conversational planning. In J. O. Greene (Ed.), *Message production: Advances in communication theory* (pp. 195-220). Mahwah, NJ: Erlbaum.

Wilson, S. R. (1997). Developing theories of persuasive message production: The next generation. In J. O. Greene (Ed.), *Message production: Advances in communication theory* (pp. 15-43). Mahwah, NJ: Erlbaum.

Wong, P. T. P. (1998). Spirituality, meaning, and successful aging. In P. T. P. Wong & P. S. Fry (Eds.) *The human quest for meaning: A handbook of psychological research and clinical applications* (pp. 359-394). Mahwah, NJ: Lawrence Erlbaum Associates, Publishers.

Zohar, D., & Marshall, I. (2000). *Connecting with our spiritual intelligence.* New York: Bloomsbury Publishing.

Chapter 3

Sparring with Spirituality
Issues of Entangling Spirituality and Communication

Kathy. L. Long
Santa Clara University

Abstract

The continued adoption and implementation of technology-supported forms of communication have many feeling that spirituality has long been removed from our everyday lives. With the beginning of a new millennium, there has been a resurgence of interest in spirituality. New technologies like the Internet are helping to support spiritual interests among individuals. The various aspects to spirituality that people engage with are embedded in communication processes. Spirituality can be viewed as coming into relationship with our experiences and reflections—a process of coming into relationship with reality (Ochs, 1983). The grounding of perceptions, beliefs, and actions within a spiritual framework requires communication researchers to consider spirituality as a factor in the communication process. Coming from a more spiritual perspective with regard to communication research allows us to go beyond the transmission mode of communicating to re-embody a more complex knowing and relationship with others and ourselves. Spiritual perspectives encompass our understanding of connection, and compel us to keep a communal, constructive perspective of meaning. This view of communication strives to reaffirm our interrelatedness, and highlights the various dimensions of reality negotiated through communication.

A s we begin a new millennium, we look to a future full of promise and trepidation. Speculating on what the world may be in the next one hundred years is not a new topic. The start of a new millennium seems to historically bring about reflection as to what has been and contemplation of what may come. Two of the "hot" topics at this time are spirituality and communication.

In the US, spiritual issues are being addressed in all facets of society. While both science and faith continue to produce "miracles" in technologies, medicine, transportation, and so on, spirituality has emerged in a range of public discourse: *Time* magazine has angels and ghosts on its covers; Oprah Winfrey creates a national angel network; Marianne Williamson chronicles everyday miracles; psychic networks promise to connect us to loved ones lost, or loved ones not yet known; Depak Chopra sells books on the mystic divinity within each of us; Scientologists fight for recognition in Germany and Hollywood; some physical scientists are promoting Gaia theory to demonstrate our connections to the universe; and New Age, Eastern, and Pagan congregations continue to grow, as does membership in most religious organizations over the last several years. In the Silicon Valley, the center for cutting-edge technology in the US (if not the world), church construction has been booming.

Not to be left behind, communication has emerged as the defining element of our modern age. New communication technologies such as fiber optic networks, high-speed computing, digital imaging, electronic data management, virtual reality, and an array of other innovations have helped to tag this period in history as the "information age" and the "communications revolution" (see Williams, 1982). More and more of us seem to be focusing our energies to create, compile, relay, and comprehend an ephemeral web of information that constitutes how we "do" our lives. We are also using these new technologies to facilitate our spiritual practices. While broadcasting channels have often been utilized by religious organizations, processing and distributing formats are providing other means by which information can be relayed to spiritual communities. Electronic mailings and newsletters, web pages, electronic bulletin boards, and desktop publishing are helping to distribute a growing body of information by and for all sorts of spiritual groups (Camp, 1996; O'Leary & Brasher, 1996; Rheingold, 1993). But communication is much more than technologies. In the last century, the scholarly field of communication has tried to establish a reputation as a legitimate academic discipline and social science (see Benson, 1985 and Rogers, 1997).

Attempting to understand the complexities and processes of communication is an ongoing challenge for communication researchers. While spirituality and communication have been highlighted as distinct issues, they are certainly interdependent constructs. Because of this interdependence, I have used the term "entangling" in order to demonstrate this interdependence. Entangling implies a meshing and weaving together so that separating distinct components becomes difficult. This is the relationship we have as a research community with spirituality and communication. This entanglement has a historical context that grounds this relationship.

In the spirit of progress

Historically, issues of spirituality have helped us make connections to self, others, and the realities we engage with. Spirituality has many connotations attached with the word itself, as well as a range of belief systems that are associated with spiritual concepts. In this sense, spirituality is not a particular belief system or religion, but rather an acknowledgment of our responsibility and connection to others and realities. Application of some general aspects of spirituality provides for a groundwork from which more specific orientations may be explored.

"In its broadest context, spirituality is being open to reality in all of its dimensions - in its rational, irrational, and super-rational complexity, and acting on that understanding" (Davis & Weaver, 1982, p. 369). Spirituality is also viewed as coming into relationship with our experiences and reflections—a process of coming into relationship with reality (Ochs, 1983). The overreaching goal of spirituality is to bring us to a greater understanding of interconnectedness, not individualization. It is through spirituality that we find a conscious, deliberate transformation of the self, others, and reality (Ochs, 1983). Thus, spirituality supports creativity, freedom, community, and wholeness.

This resurgence of spirituality comes within a historical period which some would consider non-spiritual:

> With the rise of modernism in this century, spirituality has been in retreat. Because spiritual dimensions of human activity do not seem open to observation, they are generally consigned to the realm of mythology. The enchantment of modernism derives importantly from its promise of progress—the belief that, with proper application of reason and observation, the essence of the natural world may be made increasingly known, and that with such increments in knowledge the

society may move steadily toward a utopian state. (Gergen, 1991, pp. 231-232)

Instead of spiritual perspectives determining our journey toward the ideal or utopian state, Wilson Dizard considers scientific and technological progress as the means to create a new earthly ideal. Indeed, many models of utopia, both past and present, are based on technological frameworks (Webster & Robins, 1986). Goodman (1977) notes that science and technology have been credited with liberating our spirits from superstition and traditional faiths, becoming the primary format in which we attempt to solve our problems. Yet, as Goodman points out, these same technologies are being replaced, retooled, and redesigned to remedy situations caused by previous technical applications—the application of remediation processes as noted by Gergen.

For Jacques Ellul (1964), no social, human, or spiritual fact is as important as that of technology in the modern world. It has taken over all of our everyday activities. With social advances and goals continuing to be met by technologies, the technical framework has come to assume a force of truth within our culture (Webster & Robins, 1986). Technology enables and justifies scientific knowledge, privileging it over traditional ways of knowing or over knowledge of revelation (Lyotard, 1984). Thus, it is this knowledge produced and supported by technology that is often used as the standard to determine what is true and right.

Ellul posits that technology fragments our cultural and natural realities, and recombines them to fit a technological system. Ellul claims that the world is both material and spiritual, but that technologies work to eradicate the mysterious, the magical, and the taboo. According to Ellul (1964), technology worships and respects nothing, while technicizing mystery. Even spirituality becomes "technologized" in society, and the individual is forced to become subservient to technique. Technique represents technologies - machines, as well as technical systems that may be overt or covert in our lives. These technologies combine to form a technical reality of our daily lives - technique. We are enmeshed in these technical means of life and thought. Thus, it is technique supported by technical systems that are autonomous, not people. For Ellul, it is this mystery of life, existence, and knowledge, which give us the potential for transcendence and sacredness. Encompassed by technology, we create an inhumane world of existence founded on this technicizing of our realities.

Much of our technical knowledge has been applied to communication. With the transmission metaphor of communication entrenched in many models of interaction, developing "better" ways in which messages can be sent and received has become a social imperative (see Carey, 1989). More and more of our economic and personal resources are being used to support communication technologies. As Frederick Williams (1982) suggests, our society and much of the world is in the midst of this communication revolution—instigated by the development and implementation of technologies which supports aspects of communicating. To help establish communication as a scholarly discipline has focused research toward the epistemological and phenomenological. We observe, we classify, we describe, we define, and we predict aspects of some chosen interactions. These research perspectives fit well into the modernist view of how reality is to be studied—they are very "technical". What the modernist approach does not consider is the great variety and depth of understanding that can be created through communication. The modernist view misses the ontological richness of being and interaction.

If Ellul's fears are correct, then we are merely representing the technical view of reality through the guise of spirituality. With all our new techniques, we are simply creating the appearance of spiritual practices. But on the other hand, many suggest that the role of modern technologies will be to undo the social ills previously created by these technical means (see Rheingold, 1993; Williams, 1982). Yet, innovations often have effects which are not anticipated (see Gergen, 1992; Sproull & Kiesler, 1991).

Martin Heidegger (1977) stresses that the essence of technology is not technical. He argues that technology is a way of revealing, of uncovering the truth of being. For Heidegger, our only way to get at the essence of technology is to find the full breadth of the space of essence. To achieve this, we must overcome this objectification of our reality. Objectification removes one from being and makes something merely present. This projection makes people objects and strips them from their spatial and temporal determinations. They are no longer perceived as actual or situated or real (Kockelmans, 1965, p. 119). As Heidegger contends, technology is a means to bring forth - a way to reveal these constructions which keep us from achieving our essence of being. Freedom comes from this attentive awareness and being observant of our representations and how they are reconstituted in our practice.

Hands to Work

The post-modern perspective, which considers how we construct views and contexts of reality, has helped to open the doors of research beyond the empirical and phenomenological. The resurgence of spiritual issues at a time when communication is in the forefront may not be simply a backlash to a post-industrial, modernist age. Nor, is it a new spin on this "technicized" view of culture noted by Ellul.

As suggested earlier, spirituality and communication are interdependent and share many common concepts. Take the Davis and Weaver (1982) definition used for spirituality: spirituality helps us make these connections to self, others, and the realities we engage with. Substitute "communication" for "spirituality" and the definition still works quite effectively - but, it works on a different level. Communication is the process by which we make these connections and the means by which we come to make sense of them. Because of these similarities, spirituality and communication often become merged when approached simultaneously. Spirituality and communication share many elements. Both deal with, among other things: community, understanding, ritual, interaction, connection, tradition, culture, knowing, temporality, connection, negotiation, and emotion. Spirituality is rooted in transcendence and sacredness. Communication concerns the negotiation of meaning in interaction. In some ways, communication must consistently deal with the sensual aspects of how communication is created. While transmission is one aspect of the process, it is not the only one, nor is it considered the most important (Carey, 1989). Like the complexities revealed through the study of communication, bringing communication and spirituality together within the field requires an acknowledgement of how these processes are enmeshed. One way to encourage this research is to support the sharing of research among scholars.

The National Communication Association has sponsored a series of workshops focusing specifically on issues of spirituality and communication over the last decade. In the last few years, interest in this area of research has lead to the creation of the Spiritual Communication Commission. The publications, papers and discussions at these gatherings demonstrate not only a growing interest in spirituality and communication, but also the need for the field to recognize spirituality—in its many forms—as a legitimate and compelling path of research. While religious rhetoric has long been an established area of communication research, the wider range of issues which spirituality can encompass brings greater complexity to our search for knowledge.

The term "sparring" has been intentionally used to describe how this author views the current research agenda pertaining to spirituality and communication. To spar means to practice some scripted activity, but in a safe and controlled situation. The connotation is more akin to the term applied to martial arts than to boxing. When one spars, in this sense, the goal is to master forms and to develop control. Precautions are taken so that the chance for injury is reduced while skills are honed. Yet, one must remember that it is during this practice that one becomes both student and teacher. Though a practice session is usually prescribed and contrived, these engagements have very real consequences. As communication researchers develop the skills and knowledge to uncover some of the complexities of how spirituality and communication come together, this practice also helps to reveal the realities beyond the rational and irrational into that which has come to be called "sacred".

Communication professionals are uniquely trained to analyze and make sense of how meaning is constructed. As new technologies and old spiritual practices come back into the forefront of our everyday lives, the need to understand the opportunities and realities made possible in this new age becomes more essential. I see the role of communication research in the next millennium as vital in the ethical, educational, social, and cultural realms of our everyday lives. If this post-modern, information age is about to revolutionize how we live our lives, then we have the obligation and ethical imperative to research and reveal the possibilities and consequences that these changes help us create. To ignore the spiritual aspects of our lives is to do a great disservice to the realities that we engage. For Heidegger, culture is the place where creativity and spirituality are carried out (Kockelmans, 1965). By creating a research culture that does not shy away from trying to reveal the complex relationship between issues of spirituality and communication, research helps to fulfill that obligation. Spiritual and social structures are not separate, and we must be mindful that spiritual structures can vary greatly.

Encouraging a more spiritual perspective with regard to communication research allows us to go beyond the transmission mode of communicating to re-embody a more complex knowing and relationship with others and ourselves. This acknowledges others and their essential place in the world and interaction. As James (1973) notes, "the basic unity of society, however, is the duet in which we participate with the Other" (p. 96). A spiritual perspective grounds our understanding of connection, and compels us to keep a communal perspective. This view of communication strives to reaffirm our interrelatedness, and this sharing of the world gives us all something in common.

Reintroducing a spiritual perspective to communication research also revisits those complexities that make the study of communication so challenging. Spirituality reconsiders those tireless questions of who we are, what is our place in the world, and how do we know what we know. There are still many unanswered questions concerning spirituality and communication, but it is the continued pursuit of answering these difficult questions that often leads to the best research.

References

Benson, T. (Ed.). (1985). *Speech communication in the 20ᵗʰ century*. Carbondale, IL: Southern Illinois University Press.

Camp, L. J. (1996). We are geeks, and we are not guys: The systers mailing list. In L. Cherny and E. R Weise (Eds.), *Wired women: Gender and new realities in cyberspace* (pp. 114-125). Seattle, WA: Seal Press.

Carey, J. (1989). *Communication as culture: Essays on media and society*. New York: Routledge.

Davis, J. & Weaver, J. (1982). Dimensions of spirituality. In C. Spretnak (Ed.), *The politics of women's spirituality: Essays on the rise of spiritual power within the feminist movement* (pp. 368-372). Garden City, NY: Anchor Press.

Ellul, J. (1972). *The politics of God and the politics of man* (trans. by G. Bromiley). Grand Rapids, MI: William B. Eerdmans.

Ellul, J. (1964). *The technological society* (trans. by J. Wilkinson). New York: Alfred A. Knopf.

Gergen, K. (1991). *The saturated self: Dilemmas of identity in contemporary life*. New York: Basic Books.

Gergen, K. (1996). Technology and self: From the essential to the sublime. In D. Grodin & T. Lindlof (Eds.), *Constructing the self in the mediated world* (pp. 127-140). Thousand Oaks, CA: Sage.

Goodman, P. (1977). Can technology be humane?. In A. H. Teich (Ed.), *Technology and man's future* (pp. 207-228). New York: St. Martin's Press.

James, B. (1973). *The death of progress*. New York: Alfred A. Knopf.

King, U. (1989). *Women and spirituality: Voices of protest and promise*. London: Macmillan.

Kockelmans, T. (1965). *Martin Heidegger: A first introduction to his philosophy*. Pittsburgh, PA: Dusquesne University Press.

Lyotard, J. (1984). *The post-modern condition: A report on knowledge* (trans. by G. Bennington & B. Massumi). Minneapolis, MN: University of Minnesota Press.

Mesthene, E. G. (1977). The role of technology in society. In A. H. Teich (Ed.), *Technology and man's future* (pp. 156-180). New York: St. Martin's Press.

Ochs, C. (1983). *Women and spirituality*. Totowa, NJ: Rowman & Allanheld.

O'Leary, S. D. & Brasher, B. E. (1996). The unknown God of the internet: Religious communication from the ancient agora to the virtual forum. In C. Ess (Ed.), *Philosophical perspective on computer-mediated communication* (pp. 233-269). New York: State University of New York Press.

Rheingold, H. (1993). *The virtual community: Homesteading on the electronic frontier*. Reading, MA: Addison-Wesley.

Rogers, E. (1997). *A history of communication study: A biographical approach*. New York: Simon & Schuster.

Sproull, L. & Kiesler, S. (1991). *Connections: New ways of working in the networked organization*. Cambridge, MA: MIT Press.

Webster, F. & Robins, K. (1986). *Information technology: A luddite analysis*. Norwood, NJ: Ablex.

Williams, F. (1982). *The communications revolution*. Beverly Hills, CA: Sage.

Chapter 4

Spirituality-Centered Career Theory and Practice

Patrice M. Buzzanell
Purdue University

Abstract

Rapidly changing economic circumstances have prompted individuals to reconsider the meanings of success, career, and work. In response to workforce uncertainties, individuals labor longer and harder, create their images to suit corporate and popular success prescriptions, focus on relationships as safety nets during economic downturns, and seek spirituality in their lives. Although one would think that spirituality would be safeguarded from corporate colonization, popular forms of spirituality promote corporate interests and sustain the status quo. However, we can illuminate tensions between career and spirituality in ways that enable us to reconsider the bases of our lives and develop a truly transformative spirituality-centered career theory and practice.

Spirituality-Centered Career Theory and Practice
    This essay begins by tracing the meanings of success, career, and work over the last several decades in the U.S. Rapid economic and sociopolitical changes coupled with fragmentation of traditional bases of identity and security have promoted reconsideration of our organizational attachments. One response to questions about identity, values, and instability is spirituality. Although logical that individuals would embrace spirituality in this turbulent and postmodern environment, the extent to which corporate America has welcomed spirituality deserves greater attention.

    To explore why corporate America would stress spirituality, the second part of this essay describes the corporate colonization and commodification of spirituality in the workplace. Just as conventional notions of success, career, and work operated to control workers' lives, so too have corporate spiritualities along with new career and social contracts created power imbalances that function to control our souls. By illuminating some of the underlying tensions between spirituality and career in the third section, we can lay the foundation for a spirituality-centered career theory and practice. At the conclusion of this essay, I call for a reframing of the term "career" to better meet the longings of organizational members in the U.S.

Success, Career, and Contemporary Longings for Spirituality

    In the United States, we often associate "success" with "career" and "work." Although specific details of success messages have changed over the years, we grew up hearing that ours is a land of opportunity and that, with hard work, persistence, education, and a bit of luck, we too could succeed. Success meant respectability in our communities, a nice home in a good neighborhood, intergenerational mobility, and upward advancement in organizational hierarchies (Bennett, 1991; Ciulla, 2000; Newman, 1988, 1993). Organizational career systems fostered these messages by creating early identification and tracking programs for high potential employees as well as promotion-from-within systems that encouraged people to willingly devote their lives and souls to specific companies.

    These organizational careers required employees' time, particularly during their 20s through early 40s, to accrue the knowledge, attitudes, and images required for upward movement and to signal competence and promotability. Employees, particularly white, educated, middle- or upper-class, and heterosexual males, expected these societal understanding of employer-employee arrangements (also known as psychological contracts; see Rousseau, 1995), to continue indefinitely. A sense of entitlement pervaded thinking among elite worker groups – a sense that was shattered by the new career and social contract.

This new social contract changed the discourse of career. The language of the new career and contract is focused on the inevitability of employment insecurity:

> What, then, does this suggest as a way of dealing with job insecurity? Most important is the need to remain marketable by maintaining an appropriate skill and knowledge base ... In addition, knowledge workers will need the foresight to seek out new job opportunities before short product-life cycles, restructuring, and obsolescence overtake them. ... In a market economy job security will never be a realistic goal. No amount of hard work, dedication, and loyalty will overcome the cold hand of rationality if people must be laid off. To be prepared by continuous learning and a mind set that "nothing is forever" is the best defense. (Bernstein, 1997, p. 247)

Gone were long-term relationships, loyalties, trust, and family metaphors (Buzzanell, 2000). Whereas the old career could be defined as a series of work-related experiences within and outside of organizational hierarchies that often included appearances of, if not actual, joint commitment (Arthur, Hall, & Lawrence, 1989), the new career focused on free agent mentalities and short-term exchange relationships (Byron, 1995; Chilton & Weidenbaum, 1994; Hirsch, 1987). On one hand, these transactional exchange relationships cut through the illusions of company paternalism and mutual loyalties. They potentially freed people to pursue interests other than work, organizational service, and instrumental activities geared toward corporate advancement.

On the other hand, the idea of perpetual short-term employment transactions also produced anxiety among workforce members who felt ill equipped to enact the new career (e.g., those who were less educated, lacked financial reserves to weather unemployment periods, did not tolerate ambiguity well, were unable to relocate, and so on). Little research was (and still is) conducted on the "dark side" of the new career and contract (see Hall, 1996; Sullivan, 1999). Popular and academic management materials portrayed changes optimistically (Sullivan, 1999). However, members of nondominant groups and of blue-collar occupations suffered more during economic downturns than white managerial and professional employees and often failed to gain significant and sustained advantage when the economy was doing well (see Duff, 1997; McGinn &

Naughton, 2001; U. S. General Accounting Office, 1994). In short, the new career and contract promised greater freedom to pursue economic opportunities for both parties. While organizations may have reveled in the ability to untie employment relationships when strategy, markets, ownership, and finances change, the disparity between the "haves" and the "have-nots" increased with those already privileged in our society having greater opportunities to rebound after temporary career barriers (see Buzzanell, 2000; Rifkin, 1995).

As a result of these employment relationships characterized by exchange and attendant dislocations (by time and space), many workers began to question their lives, resource allocations, and personal allegiances (Ciulla, 2000; Saltzman, 1991; Schor, 1991).[1] Workers began to respond in a variety of different ways. Some accepted job insecurity as inevitable and responded to the challenges of the new career by binding themselves more fully to work organizations. Corporate identities became their identities. Nadesan (1999b) says that corporations offered constancy: "corporate identities offer stable, paternalistic presences–so-called community structures–that transcend the individual and therefore provide the individual a locus for identification" (p. 35).

Individuals also worked in "more is better" thinking that created double binds. As fear increased, workers devoted more time, more energy, more signs of commitment, and greater adherence to corporate norms. They worked longer hours to signal commitment and to complete their projects in lean organizational structures (Perlow, 1998; see also Turnley & Feldman, 1998). They replaced their individuality with reproductions of homogenized professionalism (Nadesan, 1999b). In other words, they attempted to replicate images of athletic, attractive, well dressed, optimistic, assertive, and youthful employees supplied by popular success materials and by disciplining processes enacted by themselves and others (Nadesan, 1999b; Trethewey, 1999). How they looked and what attitudes they projected became imperative as they attempted to conform to corporate images consistent with rapidly altering global economic and sociopolitical environments.[2] They exhibited greater adherence to team norms as they paradoxically regulated themselves and others to comply with "participatory" organizing practices (see Barker, 1999; Stohl & Cheney, 2001).

Other times, they found their grounding within family, friendship, and community relationships (Kahn, 1996; Kram, 1996; Parker, 1996). This relational approach to careers attempted to situate identities within communal rather than traditional career and organizational values such as individualism, competitiveness, technical or expert rationalities, and best ways to accomplish goals (e.g., best practices, benchmarking, homogenized member images) (see Buzzanell, 1994; Gallos, 1989; Marshall, 1989; Nadesan, 1999b). Kram (1996) said that a relational approach to career development takes a holistic view of individuals and their interactions with others. Kram encourages organizations to nurture conditions that can foster a relational approach to careers. These conditions include relational values of mutuality, interdependence, and reciprocity. They also embrace worldviews that envision relationships as important sites of learning. They foster development of interpersonal competences in workforce members and opportunities to cultivate multiple developmental alliances.

Kahn (1996) took the relationship approach a step farther by asserting that organizations should be sites in which members develop secure base relationships. These caregiving relationships are based on qualities aligned with being compassionate and fully present for others. In their attachment to these trusted relational partners at work and outside of work (see Parker, 1996), individuals can find the inner resources to handle economic uncertainties and the diverse ways in which our careers unfold (see Arthur, Inkson, & Pringle, 1999).

A third route that workers took to handle the challenges of the new career and social contract involved spirituality. In this path, workers emphasized "a reality beyond the material" (Daniels, Franz, & Wong, 2000, p. 543). Spirituality connoted openness to *"an 'unseen order' in the world around us, ... the drive to create wholeness"* (Mirvis, 1997, p. 203, italics in the original). While definitions of spirituality varied from personal inner experiences of interconnectedness, through expression of qualities such as virtue and ethics in managerial behaviors, to the relationship of inner experiences and overt manifestations (Schmidt-Wilk, Heaton, & Steingard, 2000, p. 582; see also Pokora, 1996; Sass, 2000), there still was the focus on identity-creation processes guided by an inner hunger for meaning and connection.

So it is not surprising that spirituality should emerge at the end of the 20th Century as a way of transcending our plural identities and multiple employment contracts by stressing something greater than ourselves. Spirituality creates a safe haven in chaotic work environments. The linkage of spirituality and career is forged by the grounding of both processes in identity, commitment to a life path, and meaning of work (broadly defined as what we do). Spirituality has been part of ethical and servant leadership (Hickman, 1998; Greenleaf, 1996), value-driven organizing processes (Pokora, 1996; Rothschild-Whitt, 1979), and related ideas about building humane work environments (see Ciulla, 2000). In these cases, the cause, value, and moral principles underlying choices about work relationships and the communicative behaviors associated with these arrangements are what set them apart from other careers. Another distinguishing feature is that spirituality is not something that can be acquired as a career orientation, style, or strategy to enhance self and others' productivity, but is a root process of reflection, questioning, and developing self and others for a good greater than corporate survival and success.

What deserves further exploration is how and why corporate America has embraced spirituality to such a great extent (see vol. 24, issue 5, of the *Journal of Management Education*; vol. 12, issue 3, of *Journal of Organizational Change Management*; Laabs, 1995; Nadesan, 1999a; Neal, 1997). To examine these issues, we need to expose the colonization and commodification of spirituality in the workplace.

Corporate Colonization and Commodification of Spirituality

The linkages of spirituality, work, and career are not new. In prior centuries, work was associated with salvation and attempts to contribute to, rather than being a burden on, society (Bernstein, 1997). There have always been careers, called vocations or steady state paths, that are defined as growth from within and as responses to inner drives (see Arthur et al., 1999; Buzzanell & Goldzwig, 1991; Hall & Goodale, 1986; Pope, 2000). But the modern connections among work, spirituality, and career are more complex because they operate to dominate workers' minds and hearts more fully than prior forms of control. Deetz (1992) refers to this process of assuming workplace values and practices in every aspect of our lives as corporate colonization.

Because the corporate organization has become "the most central institution in modern society" (Deetz, 1992, p. ix), corporations structure our needs, educational contents and knowledge, values, reasoning, use of time, and desires for our futures. We arrange our family routines around our jobs whether we go to work or telecommute. Everything is geared toward career and organizational roles, including our educational system. Deetz says that we have choice but that once we have made our decisions, these paths and thinking then become sedimented and institutionalized to such an extent that our relationships, memberships, and other life aspects are built around and support these choices. The process is ubiquitous:

the corporate colonization of other social institutions suppresses competing identity formation and defines the context for an inner colonization whereby the individual forms the self intentionally for work relations. The corporation thus less regulates the identity rather than allows the individual to constitute it on the corporate behalf. The individual provides the construction based on limited conceptual alternatives from primarily the corporate-controlled media, in a context of corporate rewards and sanctions, and for representation in the managerial code. In this process, images enable greater systematic control and instrumental action in corporations through normalization than would be possible in simple authority relations. (Deetz, 1992, pp. 297-298)

As the individual forms an identity intentionally for work, this individual increasingly sees himself/herself as a commodity (Altman & Post, 1996). Activities once seen as enjoyable or rewarding for their own sakes now become superfluous or linked to work activities as another motivational or retention tool to sustain commitment of high performing workers (e.g., Butler & Waldroop, 1999; Ciulla, 2000; Friedman, Christensen, & DeGroot, 1998)

Besides encroaching on intrinsically enjoyable activities, corporate colonization of our lives also extends to spirituality. Some researchers have argued that spirituality and the corporate manufactured work community operate as more sophisticated ways of trying to exploit human motivations to belong, find meaning in work, and achieve self-actualization through organizational processes (see Ciulla, 2000). Nadesan (1999a) describes how corporations use spirituality to adapt individuals to new workplace arrangements. In this adaptation process, populist discourse creates images of individuals as independent agents who fashion their own environments and careers. By choosing the circumstances of their lives, engaging in therapeutic self-help, and achieving intimacy with a higher power, workforce members can attain heightened productivity and self-actualization at work. Nadesan (1999a) says that:

New Age Corporate Spiritualism is therapeutic in that it helps adapt individuals to transformed economic relations. The discourse's effectiveness stems less from its capacity for mind-control, than from its capacity to deflect attention from alternative, populist discourses that hold organizations accountable for undermining work place security, autonomy, and private lives. Individuals who attempt to bring alternative interpretations to bear are represented as taking a victim mindset. (p. 19).

In addition to New Age Corporate Spiritualism, the discourse of Evangelical Christianity (and Evangelical Capitalism in the workplace) "promises to mend the contradictions of public and private, and work and home through its ultimate vision of a new social order" (p. 21). Individuals can learn the techniques, including submission and compliance to traditional gendered roles, as routes to salvation.   Individual empowerment comes about through submission to the will of God, rejection of separation of church from state (and public from private), and articulation of beliefs in ways that appeal to mass audiences and convert new followers.   Through a personalized relationship with God and adherence to (decontextualized) Biblical precepts, individuals can achieve the kinds of self-discovery and personal growth that can enable them to sustain themselves during difficult economic times.   The challenge for workers is to adapt to—not challenge—economic relations (Nadesan, 1999a).

As spirituality becomes increasingly commercialized and commodified, we see that spirituality situates security within individuals' self-determination and abilities to adjust to rather than radically alter the workplace. Ultimately these popular forms of spirituality cannot alleviate the emptiness in our lives because they promote what is in corporations' best interests rather than what is good and true in life and relationships. Ciulla (2000) writes:

> Perhaps herein lies the key to this longing for something more. … all of these management programs have been searching for "the ghost in the machine," or a person's inner motivation, goodwill, and energy. One might call this the human spirit. But whether you call it a ghost or a spirit or internal motivation, for most of this century employers have tried to get at *it* and harness *it* to improve the productivity of their organizations. …now some consultants want to tap into the soul. … But the biggest problem is that behind this desire for spirituality often lurk serious ethical problems about how employers and employees treat each other.   In the end, spirituality at work does what pop psychology and management fads have always done: it attempts to make people *feel* good and adapt, not address the serious problems of power, conflict, and autonomy that make people feel bad in the first place. (pp. 222-223, italics in original)

To develop a spirituality-based career theory and practice in the conclusion of this essay, the tensions between spirituality and career need to be exposed in the next section.

Tensions Between Spirituality and Career

Writing about spirituality and career seems contradictory epistemologically, ontologically, and axiologically. Our ways of knowing spiritually derive from the deep longings of our souls to find personal and communal meaning and may (or may not) coincide with religious traditions. Our spiritual understandings of being constitute our ephemeral, infinite, joyful turn inward – separate from, yet intimately related to, our physical senses and the communities to which we belong. Our spiritual values reflect what we and others believe is worthy in life—usually to live ethically and to develop wisdom that can guide our actions and help others learn. When these spiritual aspects of ourselves coincide with our actions, we find deep peace. Spirituality is seated in the ideal and idealistic, although spirituality often is manifest in good works and relationships to community.[3]

In spirituality, community with others is central to living. Daniels et al. (2000) state that an "implication of valuing community is the recognition that we do not exist in isolation but are part of a larger entity. Being in community entails certain responsibilities, both toward other people and toward our organizations and environments" (p. 557). These responsibilities involve treating ourselves and others with dignity and respect and serving a vision of lives that transcend their material aspects. Whether we call these responsibilities servant leadership (Graham, 1991; Greenleaf, 1996), feminist visions of serving (Fine & Buzzanell, 2000), ethics (Held, 1993), or some other label, the sense is that the work of spirituality is to both deepen connection with higher order (such as a God, or inner light) and integrate these understandings into our everyday relationships.

In contrast, career connotes the public world of work, employment, and materiality. Career typically prioritizes knowing through technical expertise (see Belenky, Clinchy, Goldberger, & Tarule, 1986; Mumby & Stohl, 1996), outward displays of oneself and one's outputs as noteworthy (Buzzanell & Goldzwig, 1991), and values of work as contribution to external goals (i.e., personal livelihood, need fulfillment, and organizational goals) as well as self expression and self actualization (Bernstein, 1997; Ciulla, 2000). Career motivation is pragmatic, with individual action being the principal means of marking achievement of short- and long-term goals. Agency, "the ability of actors (persons, groups, firms, stockholders) to make decisions and to act out of their own interests" (Rousseau & Arthur, 1999, p. 8; see also Marshall, 1989, 1995), forms the basis of traditional career. To act in one's best interests often self against others in adversarial relationships as one needs to distinguish oneself, to compete and win in the "survival of the fittest" context (see Buzzanell & Goldzwig, 1991; Newman, 1993). The construct of career serves organizational needs by presumably motivating workers to signal loyalty, commitment, and promotability.

Although we can say that action taken to further one's success and employability underlies career theory and practice, agency still is constrained by corporate imperatives and colonization that create a seamless union of organizational and personal goals, identities, and justices (see Deetz, 1992, 1995; Scott & Hart, 1989). The responsibilities of career are to serve the employing organization and to create a vision or Dream in early career phases that can motivate or drive us toward success (see Levinson, 1978, 1996; Scott & Hart, 1989). The Dream is occupationally – not spiritually – oriented (Kittrell, 1999); the Dream also is self – not community – focused (Gothard, 1999). The Dream is linearly drawn, whereas spirituality and community are ongoing, never-ending processes that transcend space and time.

Career time is grounded in specific spatial and temporal dimensions (see Arthur et al., 1989) and can be punctuated by various milestones. Even the retrospective construction of career narratives is a self- and work-oriented construction of linearity that merges past with future goals (e.g., Arthur et al., 1999; Komisar, 2000). These stories string together life events through an unfolding understanding of personal life interests or themes.

In short, the ways of knowing, being, valuing, experiencing space and time, and relating to self and others differ in career and spirituality. Yet, both constructs center on who we are and want to be individually and organizationally (see Pokora, 1996, for links between spirituality and organizational identification). Both begin with "know thyself." In career theory, self-knowledge may come from vocational assessments, career counseling, and reviewing one's work experiences for themes (see Arthur et al., 1999; Holland, 1996, Muchinsky, 1999). In spirituality, Barnett, Krell, and Sendry (2000) advocate teaching that encourages students to answer questions such as "What does it mean to be a spiritual person? What is spirituality? What are the causes and consequences? How does spirituality develop, and when?" (p. 563).

Of importance in reframing career to ask questions such as "How can we infuse career theory and practice with spirituality – not as something added on – but a quality whereby we construct our lives? Is it possible to develop spirituality-centered career discourse that can sustain questioning of corporate colonization and commodification of our lives? What forces mitigate against development and implementation of a spirituality-centered career theory and practice? What can we do to lessen the effectiveness of these forces?"

Reframing Career: A Spirituality-Centered Career Theory and Practice

Here I am, Lord.
Is it I, Lord?
I have heard you calling in the night.
I will go, Lord.
If you lead me.
I will hold your people in my heart. (Isaiah 6)

In this section, I create a spirituality-centered career theory and practice by using spirituality as an analytic lens to locate what may be missing in career theorizing and to put these understandings into our theorizing, consulting, and teaching.

Krone (2000) uses spirituality as an analytic method for deriving different meanings of work. She broadens "work" to include inner work as a "range of ways to access and cultivate spirit, and as a necessary step toward the recovery and articulation of suppressed experience" (p. 2). Spirituality is coming to know more deeply who we are. Using creation spirituality, the conceptualization of life as a spiritual journey integrating paths of pain, creativity, joy/wonder, and transformation, Krone (2000) reconceptualizes four organizational communication processes (message production, role negotiation, framing/re-framing, and discursive closure) through spirituality. What is interesting is that Krone says that she is overlaying spirituality to see what might emerge differently in organizational communication but, if spirituality is coming to know ourselves more fully, then she is doing more than utilizing spirituality as an analytic method. She is trying to figure out how to engage in thinking that fundamentally alters organizational communication as a discipline by positioning values and meaning of work, life, and community as both processes and outcomes.

Just as Krone reconsiders work through a spiritual lens, so too can we reconsider career in this manner. As noted earlier, traditional notions of career, work, and employment consolidate our daily patterns and identities around others' opinions rather than from inner and community commitments. Traditional career provides us with answers for why we do what we do—even when the answers surface retrospectively (Arthur et al., 1999). Career gives sense and ordering to daily work processes but also constrains us temporally so that we often lack the time (or do not consider taking the time) to reflect on what is happening to us and who we are.

Thus, spirituality-centered career theory and practice consists of three transformative processes: (a) reevaluating the ways we do time, (b) living values that are cornerstones for spirituality, and (c) locating specific ways to infuse our everyday practices with spirituality. *Time* is the critical factor in the enactment of spirituality-centered careers. Ciulla (2000) is correct then when she says that:

> If employers want to fill this need for something more, the answer is not in a prayer meeting or a seminar on finding your soul. They need to rethink the structure of the workplace and give employees more time and flexibility to lead good lives outside of work without fear of losing promotions, bonuses, or jobs. But employers are not the only ones to blame. Many employees have gotten lazy and willingly let their employers take responsibility for parts of their lives. (p. 224)

However, the issue is that time typically is bounded, regulated, and adapted to corporate needs. Career fills our time and can hinder our imagination. Career directs our attention to measurable outputs of energy expenditures, meeting attendance, report writing, and so on. We spend our days doing what supposedly has to be done and do not find sustained time or even moments for reflection. Even our leisure time is filled with mass-produced images, summer camps (preparation for our children's future careers so that they have the edge over someone else), television, shopping at malls, and other activities. The American family is "busy every minute and proud of it, too" (Shellenbarger, 2000, p. B1). Doing something, keeping busy, being involved in activities, looking forward to the career future–all these daily performances mean that someone else or something else drives our routines. And mindless routine and time expenditure are antithetical to spirituality.

Spirituality is about questioning and living with our ideals and values (Harlos, 2000; Mirvis, 1997). Spirituality also is transcendence from mundane minutiae of life (Csikszentmihalyi, 1997; Pokora, 1996) and examination of our souls on a daily basis. We can accomplish some of the work of spirituality alone but cannot fulfill our spirituality without others. Whereas the hallmarks of career are movement (in work content, learning, and advancement), adherence to corporate best interests, and individualism, Harlos (2000) adapts Neal's (1997) spiritual principles to set the cornerstones of spirituality:

> humility, compassion, and simplicity. When we center ourselves around humility, we display a healthy resistance to toxic levels of arrogance and ego that can hinder learning. When we are humble, we are not *the* member of a group but *a* member; humility fosters a sense of community in the classroom [and other organizational settings] by helping to create an atmosphere of shared responsibility for learning [and other goals]. (Harlos, 2000, pp. 617-618)

Humility means that we do not orient our lives toward placement in competitive situations that produce winners and losers. By not gearing action toward external self-recognition, humility often centers on choices that contradict conventional career wisdom. Yet, spirituality and traditional career success do not need to be antithetical. Those who practice humility may reach top corporate offices such as Chief Executive Officer (CEO), the pinnacle of external career success. These "level five" leaders combine humility with a fierce resolve to change their corporations (Collins, 2001). They are guided by the needs of others and often divert attention away from themselves as individuals.

Besides humility, compassion marks spirituality-centered career theory and enactment. Instead of sustaining corporate imperatives that are not in our best interests (e.g., the corporate survival is of greatest concern, shareholders are the ultimate stakeholder, layoffs are necessary evils), we operate with compassion. Compassion is "a deep concern for others expressed as helpful, kind actions requiring empathy, patience, and courage" (Harlos, 2000, p. 618; see also Kahn, 1996). When we are spiritually centered, we question everyday actions and structures that are produced and reproduced by organizational members' communication (e.g., micropractices and structures, such as recruitment, retention, and compensation). We also conduct research and derive practices that are designed to lessen the adverse material conditions that suck hope out of the most vulnerable members of our society (e.g., Weinger, 1998).

Finally, simplicity encourages us to "focus on substantive, significant issues rather than on superficial, irrelevant appearances" (Harlos, 2000, p. 619). In our discipline of organizational communication, we have a rich history of simplicity. The call to focus on what underlies our research, teaching, theory, and consulting, particularly our belief systems and values, have remained a continual refrain from our most prominent scholars (e.g., Redding, 1979, 1984, 1985, 1996). When we focus on what people contribute to the well-being of a community and what really matters in life, then we strip away superficial demands and issues.

These three cornerstones of humility, compassion, and simplicity are missing from traditional career theory and practice. Even when we talk about career as evolving stories of our work lives, we focus on individual sense-making within cultural narrative and myths (e.g., Arthur et al., 1999; Gothard, 1999). We have career models that focus on developmental learnings that must be achieved before we can cycle into other life phases (see Arthur et al., 1999; Salomone, 1996; Levinson, 1978, 1996), but these are not infused with spirituality. They are not associated with a higher power, an ongoing questioning of life's purposes and our part in this spiritual plan, or community. We fail to discuss career processes that can develop and move human beings to greatness.[4]

The third transformative process is *locating specific ways to infuse our everyday practices with spirituality.* First, we can communicate in ways that model the three values in spirituality. For instance, compassion means that there is a genuine commitment to reach into the resources of our beings and our community to challenge micropractices, employment arrangements, and common understandings of the ordinary ways of accomplishing work and careers (e.g., Buzzanell, 2000). Compassion manifests itself in community-enhancing rather than communication-diminishing behaviors (Buzzanell, 1995). Community-enhancing communication includes discourse that situates decision making within context, messages within priorities of relationship, and celebrations within an ongoing development of greater understanding of diverse members' lives. Ciulla (2000) comments that we can make a difference in daily acts:

> On a day-to-day basis most jobs can't fill the tall order of making the world better, but particular incidents at work have meaning because you make a valuable contribution or you are able to genuinely help someone in need or you come up with a creative solution to a difficult problem. These meaningful acts are distinctive because people do them with a good will and not for the sake of a paycheck. … Such moments fill valuable lives. (p. 226)

In contrast to community-building and meaningful micropractices, community-diminishing strategies include patronizing behaviors, outgroup language for boundary maintenance, humor that deflects talk from issues causing concern among some members, and strategies that subordinate, exclude, manipulate, and deceive (see Buzzanell, 1995; Redding, 1996). Gaining awareness of how our daily behaviors enhance or constrain community processes assists spirituality. Development of deeper compassion is as much a career maturation resource as networking and mentoring. As a resource, compassion enables us to sustain personal slights and develop a secure base for the inevitable uncertainties in our careers.

Second, we can unleash time from organizational constraints. We need to question organizational routines that take time unnecessarily. To engage in this kind of questioning means that we suspend time to take a critical look at everything we do. From a business perspective, this scrutiny is called working smarter, not harder, and establishing priorities. From a spirituality-based standpoint, this questioning can be considered the process by which we locate the meaning of work and whether different activities fulfill some greater purpose than filling time.

In addition, we also need to find the means within ourselves and through the help of others to dissociate organizational concerns and work problems from our thoughts. Unless we can empty our minds of work-related thoughts, we cannot be fully present for others. We must establish organizational procedures, especially reward systems, that overtly value time spent challenging the everyday practices of our organization lives and time spent assisting others.

Ultimately, the spirituality-centered career is threatening to corporations because this career locates time, agency, meaning, and identity within a combination of the individual, a higher power or value in life, and community. If individuals truly are centered spiritually, then their identities and their spirituality cannot be coopted by the organization. They may love their work, enjoy accomplishing work goals, and spend time thinking about challenging work problems—but they engage in these work behaviors with conscious choice. They recognize that the basis of their decision making is humility, compassion, and simplicity. If they find themselves serving the corporation and the status quo to the detriment of their spirits and other people, then they either work toward changing the system or they leave. They realize that if the basis of their decisions is within their souls and their relationships with others, then their choices may mean job loss and fewer material resources, but greater flexibility in what they can and would do.

Finally, we can apply principles of humility, compassion, and simplicity in the methods and content of our teaching. For over a decade, I have been teaching career issues and development in week-long seminars to engineers, engineering managers, and top officers. Participants change over the years but their concerns remain the same. There's the 45-year-old male engineers who remarks, "when will I know who I want to be when I grow up?" There's the woman who fears telling people at work about her partner for any number of reasons. There's the 30-something father of three who questions whether an anticipated promotion and concomitant relocation is what he really wants. There's the female project manager who is tired of answering questions about why she isn't home with her children despite public knowledge of her stay-at-home partner and her fast track status (and enjoyment of work-related challenges) in her corporation. There's the guy in his late 20s who has just been informed that he is going to hold meetings with his direct reports about what they want to do in their careers (and is scared to death because he feels that there is nothing in his background that has prepared him for dealing with people rather than technical problems). There's the engineer waiting for retirement so that he can pursue the work about which he dreams—teaching.

In these executive education seminars as well as in my graduate and undergraduate career seminars, we begin by filling out a survey. This survey asks participants about their career stories, metaphors, best and worse experiences (and lessons learned), advice for newcomers, hopes for their futures, fantasies about alternative work, sources of career information, and so on. Every year, the survey changes as career issues in the workplace and career research evolve. However, the usual response over the years has been that the questionnaire was difficult to do, could have taken days, caused them to think, and needed to be revisited as they learned more about themselves in relation to others. In my current graduate seminar, several participants remarked that they didn't know that other graduate students shared their uncertainties, their love of teaching, their joy of learning, and their hopes for their futures.

In a way, completing these surveys enable seminar participants to suspend time. Filling out the survey gives participants permission to claim time to think about their lives, their present situations, and their futures. Their responses are a gift to themselves and to others. In our seminars, we interpret our own and others' survey responses and we look at the power of language and of corporate imperatives (even in interorganizational careers and non-organizationally based careers) to draw boundaries around our identities. We find community in our seminars as we collaboratively create greater understandings of ourselves and others, of our readings, and of other materials that we bring into seminar discussions. We describe risks—risks associated with different career actions, with working toward authenticity in work-life, and with interrogating current career practices. These career seminars are not safe journeys. The discussions contain different kinds of learnings for different participants—learnings that I cannot anticipate fully but that I can facilitate by opening the conversation for exploration.

Kirkwood (1994) worried that spiritual talk might set up spirit/matter or spiritual/nonspiritual life dualisms that can minimize the material concerns of our lives and those who choose not to emphasize the spiritual. Yet, there is no reason to promote or adhere to such a bifurcation. The spiritual is a root process underlying what we do whether we call it spirituality or some other term. If we focus less on the external trappings of career and more on the inner and community-enhancing processes, we have an opportunity to build career understandings that truly are innovative. Surveys indicate that across the globe, people strive for congruence in their lives and meaning in their work (see Laabs, 1995). They welcome values-centered approaches and time for reflection to create greater consistency between spirituality and actions. The spirituality-centered career can transform the communicative processes in our workplace as well as address our ongoing needs for meaning.

Notes

[1]There are other reasons why individuals were questioning themselves, others, and the institutions to which they belonged (or aspired to gain membership). Nadesan (1999b) notes that "post-modern conditions engender multiple possibilities for the proliferation of heterogeneous social discourses and the concomitant creative exploration of identities, [while] they also generate angst as individuals strive vainly to provide secure foundations for their identity" (p. 31). Deetz (1992) notes that individuals have shifted identities to work and career without realizing the full implications of these processes. He states that the origin of identity has changed from family and community organizations to a more constraining identity that serves corporate rather than individual interests. It is an illusion that we can construct an autonomous self-determined self within our corporate identities.

[2]I do not wish to imply that anyone who enacts the image of an organization or who works long hours is spiritually vacuous or superficial. What I do want to suggest is that corporate imperatives and their consequences dominate our thinking, acting, behaving, and feeling to such an extent that we often do not reflect on the who we are and how our actions contradict what we profess to value (see Deetz, 1992, 1995; Hochschild, 1997).

In addition, the three ways in which individuals handle the new career and social contract (i.e., by doing more, by locating security within relationships, and by "finding" spirituality) are not mutually exclusive and exhaustive categories. Rather, they are trends that individuals may choose to enact depending on their career anchors (i.e., fairly stable life interests noticeable after individuals have been in the workforce for several years; Schein, 1992), life interests (Butler & Waldroop, 1999; Friedman et al., 1998), personality proclivities (see Tieger & Barron-Tieger, 1995), developmental needs during career and life phases (e.g., Arthur et al., 1999; Levinson, 1978, 1996) and the materials realities of their lives (Buzzanell, 2000).

[3]This essay focuses on spirituality as a life-sustaining force. However, there are numerous variations in spirituality as designed and practiced. An opposing perspective on spirituality could argue that this uniformly positive presentation of spirituality submerges the dark unseen order that also can stress something greater than ourselves. The contrast between and tensions within ourselves as we search for self and community between the dialectics of wholeness and separation, good and evil, and truths and falsehoods provide us with greater understanding of why and how spirituality is so important and so difficulty to achieve in our daily lives.

[4]Perhaps we have not developed these kinds of career programs because we really do not know how to "train" people toward spiritually-centered corporate careers. Most leadership and career research and practice are geared toward training models (as are many self-help popular media materials and standardized corporate spirituality programs, such as those mentioned by Nadesan, 1999a). Collins (2001) questions whether "level five" leaders can be "taught." Their discussion centers on these leaders' memorable life experiences and desires not to

focus attention on themselves. They claim that these leaders are "born" and not "made." Yet, childhood and other experiences provide the grounding for development of spiritually-centered career processes and understandings. Uncovering how individuals find meaning and spirituality throughout their lives is one direction that communication research can take. Two sites for investigating spiritually-centered careers and decision processes are within religious and value-rational organizations (e.g., Pokora, 1996) and within self-identified crises in individuals' and communities' lives.

References

Altman, B. W., & Post, J. E. (1996). Beyond the "social contract": An analysis of the executive view at twenty-five large companies. In D. T. Hall & Associates (Eds.), *The career is dead - Long live the career: A relational approach to careers* (pp. 46-71). San Francisco: Jossey-Bass.

Arthur, M. B., Hall, D. T., & Lawrence, B. S. (1989). Generating new directions in career theory: The case for a transdisciplinary approach. In M. B. Arthur, D. T. Hall, & B. S. Lawrence (Eds.), *Handbook of career theory* (pp. 7-25). Cambridge: Cambridge University Press.

Arthur, M. B., Inkson, K., & Pringle, J. K. (1999). *The new careers: Individual action and economic change.* London: Sage.

Barker, J. (1999). *The discipline of teamwork: Participation and concertive control.* Thousand Oaks, CA: Sage.

Barnett, C. K., Krell, T. C., & Sendry, J. (2000). Learning to learn about spirituality: A categorical approach to introducing the topic into management courses. *Journal of Management Education, 24,* 562-579.

Belenky, M. F., Clinchy, B. M., Goldberger, N. R., & Tarule, J. M. (1986). *Women's ways of knowing: The development of self, voice, and mind.* New York: BasicBooks.

Bennett, A. (1991). *The death of the organization man.* New York: William Morrow & Co., Inc.

Bernstein, P. (1997). *American work values: Their origin and development.* Albany: State University of New York Press.

Butler, T., & Waldroop, J. (1999). Job sculpting: The art of retaining your best people. *Harvard Business Review, 77* (5), 144-152.

Buzzanell, P. M. (1994). Gaining a voice: Feminist perspectives in organizational communication. *Management Communication Quarterly, 7,* 339-383.

Buzzanell, P. M. (1995). Reframing the glass ceiling as a socially constructed process: Implications for understanding and change. *Communication Monographs, 62,* 327-354.

Buzzanell, P. M. (2000). The promise and practice of the new career and social contract: Illusions exposed and suggestions for reform. In P. M. Buzzanell (Ed.), *Rethinking organizational and managerial communication from feminist perspectives* (pp. 209-235). Thousand Oaks, CA: Sage.

Buzzanell, P. M., & Goldzwig, S. R. (1991). Linear and nonlinear career models: Metaphors, paradigms, and ideologies. *Management Communication Quarterly, 4,* 466-505.

Byron, W. J. (1995). Coming to terms with the new corporate

contract. *Business Horizons, 38* (1), 8-15.

Chilton, K., & Weidenbaum, M. (1994). *A new social contract for the American workplace: From paternalism to partnering.* St. Louis, MO: Center for the study of American business.

Ciulla, J. (2000). *The working life: The promise and betrayal of modern work.* New York: Crown Publishing Group.

Collins, J. (2001). Level 5 leadership: The triumph of humility and fierce resolve. *Harvard Business Review, 79* (1), 66-76.

Csikszentmihalyi, M. (1997). *Finding flow: The psychology of engagement with everyday life.* New York: BasicBooks.

Daniels, D., Franz, R. S., & Wong, K. (2000). A classroom with a worldview: Making spiritual assumptions explicit in management education. *Journal of Management Education, 24,* 540-561.

Deetz, S. A. (1992). *Democracy in the age of corporate colonization: Developments in communication and the politics of everyday life.* Albany: State University of New York Press.

Deetz, S. A. (1995). *Transforming communication, transforming business: Building responsive and responsible workplaces.* Cresskill, NJ: Hampton.

Duff, C. (1997, June 3). Surging economy bypasses black men: Blue-collar workers face particularly daunting odds. *Wall Street Journal,* p. A2, A4.

Fine, M., & Buzzanell, P. M. (2000). Walking the high wire: Leadership theorizing, daily acts, and tensions. In P. M. Buzzanell (Ed.), *Rethinking organizational and managerial communication from feminist perspectives* (pp. 128-156). Thousand Oaks, CA: Sage.

Friedman, S. D., Christensen, P., & DeGroot, J. (1998). Work and life: The end of the zero-sum game. *Harvard Business Review, 76* (6), 119-129.

Gallos, J. V. (1989). Exploring women's development: Implications for career theory, practice, and research. In M. B. Arthur, D. T. Hall, & B. S. Lawrence (Eds.), *Handbook of career theory* (pp. 110-132). Cambridge: Cambridge University Press.

Gothard, B. (1999). Career as a myth. *Psychodynamic Counseling,* 5 (1), 87-97.

Graham, J. W. (1991). Servant-leadership in organizations: Inspirational and moral. *Leadership Quarterly, 2,* 105-119.

Greenleaf, R. K. (1996). *On becoming a servant leader.* San Francisco: Jossey-Bass.

Hall, D. T. (1996). Long live the career: A relational approach. In

68 Essays on Communication & Spirituality

D. T. Hall & Associates (Eds.), *The career is dead - Long live the career: A relational approach to careers* (pp. 1-14). San Francisco: Jossey-Bass.

Hall, D. T., & Goodale, J. G. (1986). *Human resource management: Strategy, design, and implementation.* Glenview, IL: Scott, Foresman & Co.

Harlos, K. P. (2000). Toward a spiritual pedagogy: Meaning, practice, and applications in management education. *Journal of Management Education, 24,* 612-627.

Held, V. (1993). Feminist morality: Transforming culture, society, and politics. Chicago: University of Chicago Press.

Hickman, G. (Ed.). (1998). *Leading organizations: Perspectives for a new era.* Thousand Oaks, CA: Sage.

Hirsch, P. (1987). *Pack your own parachute: How to survive mergers, takeovers, and other corporate disasters.* Reading, MA: Addison-Wesley.

Hochschild, A. (1997). *The time bind: When work becomes home and home becomes work.* New York: Metropolitan Books.

Holland, J. L. (1996). Exploring careers with a typology: What we have learned and some new directions. *American Psychologist, 51,* 397-406.

Isaiah. (1994). Here I am, Lord. In R. J. Batastrini & M. A. Cymbala (Eds.), *Gather Comprehensive* (#686). Chicago: GIA Publishers, Inc.

Kahn, W. A. (1996). Secure base relationships at work. In D. T. Hall & Associates (Eds.), *The career is dead - Long live the career: A relational approach to careers* (pp. 158-179). San Francisco: Jossey-Bass.

Kirkwood. W. G. (1994). Studying communication about spirituality and the spiritual consequences of communication. *The Journal of Communication and Religion, 17* (1), 13-26.

Kittrell, D. (1998). A comparison of the evolution of men's and women's dreams in Daniel Levinson's Theory of Adult Development. *Journal of Adult Development, 5,* 105-115.

Komisar, R. (2000). Goodbye career, hello success. *Harvard Business Review, 78 (*2), 161-162.

Kram, K. E. (1996). A relational approach to career development. In D. T. Hall & Associates (Eds.), *The career is dead - Long live the career: A relational approach to careers* (pp. 132-157). San Francisco: Jossey-Bass.

Krone, K. (2000, April). *Reframing organizational communication theory and research through spirituality*. Paper presented at the Central States Communication Association conference, held in Detroit, MI.

Laabs, J. J. (1995). Balancing spirituality and work. *Personnel Journal, 74* (9), 60-76.

Levinson, D. J. (1978). *The seasons of a man's life.* New York: Alfred A. Knopf.

Levinson, D. J. (1996). *The seasons of a woman's life.* New York: Alfred A. Knopf.

Marshall, J. (1989). Re-visioning career concepts: A feminist invitation. In M. B. Arthur, D. T. Hall, & B. S. Lawrence (Eds.), *Handbook of career theory* (pp. 275-291). Cambridge, MA: Cambridge University Press.

Marshall, J. (1995). *Women managers moving on: Exploring career and life choices.* London: Routledge.

McGinn, D., & Naughton, K. (2001, February 5). How safe is your job? *Newsweek, 137* (6), 36-43.

Mirvis, P. H. (1997). "Soul work" in organizations. *Organization Science, 8,* 193-206.

Muchinsky, P. M. (1999). Applications of Holland's theory in industrial and organizational settings. *Journal of Vocational Behavior, 55,* 127-135.

Mumby, D., & Stohl, C. (1996). Disciplining organizational communication studies. *Management Communication Quarterly, 10,* 50-72.

Nadesan, M. H. (1999a). The discourses of corporate spiritualism and evangelical capitalism. *Management Communication Quarterly, 13,* 3-42.

Nadesan, M. H. (1999b). The popular success literature and "A brave new Darwinian workplace." *Consumption, Markets and Culture, 3,* 27-60.

Neal, J. A. (1997). Spirituality in management education: A guide to resources. *Journal of Management Education, 21,* 121-139.

Newman, K. S. (1988). *Falling from grace: The experience of downward mobility in the American middle class.* New York: The Free Press.

Newman, K. S. (1993). *Declining fortunes: The withering of the American dream.* New York: BasicBooks.

Parker, V. A. (1996). Growth-enhancing relationships outside work (GROWs). In D. T. Hall & Associates (Eds.), *The career is dead - Long live the career: A relational approach to careers* (pp. 180-195). San Francisco: Jossey-Bass.

Perlow, L. A. (1998). Boundary control: The social ordering of work and family time in a high-tech corporation. *Administrative Science Quarterly, 43,* 328-357.

Pokora, R. M. (1996). *"And Mary danced": Communication and spirituality at a women's religious organization.* Unpublished dissertation. Purdue University.

Pope, M. (2000). A brief history of career counseling in the United States. *Career Development Quarterly, 48* (3), 194-211.

Redding, W. C. (1979). Organizational communication theory and ideology: An overview. In D. Nimmo (Ed.), *Communication yearbook 3* (pp. 309-341). New Brunswick, NJ: Transaction.

Redding, W. C. (1984). *The corporate manager's guide to better communication.* Glenview, IL: Scott, Foresman and Co.

Redding, W. C. (1985). Rocking boats, blowing whistles, and teaching speech communication. *Communication Education, 34,* 245-258.

Redding, W. C. (1996). Ethics and the study of organizational communication: When will we wake up? In J. A. Jaksa & M. S. Pritchard (Eds.), *Responsible communication: Ethical issues in business, industry, and the professions* (pp. 17-40). Cresskill, NJ: Hampton.

Rifkin, J. (1995). *The end of work: The decline of the global labor force and the dawn of the post-market era.* New York: Jeremy P. Tarcher/Putnam.

Rothschild-Whitt, J. (1979). The collectivist organization: An alternative to rational-bureaucratic models. *American Sociological Review, 44,* 509-527.

Rousseau, D. M. (1995). *Psychological contracts in organizations: Understanding written and unwritten agreements.* Thousand Oaks, CA: Sage.

Rousseau, D. M., & Arthur, M. B. (1999). Building agency and community in the new economic era. *Organizational Dynamics, 27* (4), 7-18.

Salomone, P. R. (1996). Tracing Super's theory of vocational development: A 40-year retrospective. *Journal of Career Development, 22,* 167-184.

Saltzman, A. (1991). *Downshifting: Reinventing success on a slower track.* New York: HarperCollinsPublishers.

Sass, J. S. (2000). Characterizing organizational spirituality: An organizational communication culture approach. *Communication Studies,*

51, 195-217.

Schein, E. H. (1992). Career anchors and job/role planning: The links between career planning and career development. In D. H. Montross & C. J. Shinkman (Eds.), *Career development: Theory and practice* (pp. 207-218). Springfield, IL: Charles C. Thomas.

Schmidt-Wilk, J., Heaton, D. P., & Steingard, D. (2000). Higher education for higher consciousness: Haharishi University of Management as a model for spirituality in management education. *Journal of Management Education, 24,* 580-611.

Schor, J. B. (1991*). The overworked American: The unexpected decline of leisure.* New York: BasicBooks.

Scott, W. G., & Hart, D. K. (1989). *Organizational values in America.* New Brunswick, NJ: Transaction.

Shellenbarger, S. (2000, August 16). The American family: Busy every minute and proud of it, too. *Wall Street Journal,* p. B1.

Stohl, C., & Cheney, G. (2001). Participatory processes/paradoxical practices: Communication and the dilemmas of organizational democracy. *Management Communication Quarterly, 14,* 349-407.

Sullivan, S. E. (1999). The changing nature of careers: A review and research agenda. *Journal of Management, 25,* 457-484.

Tieger, P. D., & Barron-Tieger, B. (1995). *Do what you are: Discover the perfect career for you through the secrets of personality type* (2nd ed.). Boston: Little, Brown & Co.

Trethewey, A. (1999). Isn't it ironic: Using irony to explore the contradictions of organizational life. *Western Journal of Communication, 63,* 140-167.

Turnley, W. H., & Feldman, D. C. (1998). Psychological contract violations during corporate restructuring. *Human Resource Management, 37* (1), 71-83.

U. S. General Accounting Office. (1994, September). *Equal employment opportunity: Displacement rates, unemployment spells, and reemployment wages by race* (GAO-HEHS Publication No. 94-229FS). Washington, DC: Health, Education, and Human Services Division.

Weinger, S. (1998). Children living in poverty: Their perception of career opportunities. *Families in Society: The Journal of Contemporary Human Services, 79,* 320-330.

Chapter 5

Spirituality and Aesthetics:
Embracing Nàrrative Theory

Robin Patric Clair
Purdue University

Abstract

The proposition that narrative theory may be advanced, refined, or altered, in some way by exposing it to spirituality and aesthetics is explored in this chapter. A brief review of narrative theory is followed by a discussion of the spiritually-driven work of three contemporary scholars—Harlos (2000), Gonzalez (2000), and Clair (1998) for their impact and the implications concerning the study of narrative especially in relation to Native American perspectives.

I am neither a religious person nor a terribly spiritual person. Yet, I was asked to contribute to this volume. As a matter of fact, I must admit that several years ago when one of my colleagues confronted me at a national conference and posed the following: "We should do a panel on spirituality and work," I actually cringed. "No," she assured me, "it's not what you're thinking."

I am not sure how my friend and colleague was so sure that she knew what I was thinking, but let's assume that she did. If she could read my mind, then she would have found a mixture of messages. In a culture dominated by Judeo-Christians, I immediately worried about the Christian influence about to permeate my workplace. Although I was reared as a Roman Catholic (my Dad was more likely to describe us as Irish Catholics), I have no love loss for organized religion. They have done as much bad as good in the world. I left "The Church" at age 15. I rather like that our government attempts to separate church and state; and, in most cases, this ideal is practiced in the workplace. I prefer not to face other people's religion at work. Perhaps, this is what my friend thought I was thinking when she said "No, it's not what you're thinking." But that was not all that I was thinking.

I am of mixed ancestry. My mother is of French and Cherokee heritage. My mother and my grandmothers before her (on my Cherokee side) have changed religions to complement their husband's religion for generations. The earliest grandmother that I have knowledge of was a traditional Cherokee woman. She married a white man and attended two "Meetings," but no note of her conversion is documented in family records. However, as the missionaries made their presence more and more permanent in the South, many Cherokee joined Christian faiths (e.g., Moravian, Baptist, Methodist). My mother's mother joined the Church of Christ. My mother converted to Catholicism after meeting my father. Thus, the idea that there is one true religion(as encouraged by my father's opinions) seems a debatable statement (as exemplified by my mother and grandmother's religious choices).

Although my parents religiously (pun intended) attended Mass on Sundays and tried to be good Catholics, they were not confined by Catholicism. They often allowed themselves the freedom to pursue New Age endeavors such as transcendental meditation (TM).[1] And they made sure that each of us (my seven siblings and myself) received a mantra and had the time and place to meditate. I suspect that most of the New Age introductions came from my mother's suggestions. She always seemed to me to be spiritually motivated (albeit it is my father who continues TM to this day). My mother taught me that all people are beautiful, that the earth and all her creatures are connected within the web of life. She found no harm in thanking the plants that we pluck from the earth. Her rules were more philosophical and less bureaucratically organized and mandated than those of most organized religions (e.g., when I was a child, the Catholic Church 's rules included abstaining from eating meat on Fridays, fasting before taking the Eucharist, no skipping church on Sunday, etc). I prefer the relaxed style over the more stringent and structured style of engaging the Great Spirit.

Some people suggest that my Native American heritage privileges my knowledge of spiritual matters. This is a New Age revelation grounded, in part, in stereotypes. A New Age perspective encourages seeking a sense of fulfillment. A variety of approaches are offered from transcendental meditation to Tavistock; from medicine bundles to reiki. Others seek New Age spirituality from book shelves. They gather up the old (e.g., Siddhartha by Hermen Hesse (1922/1999) or Zen and the Art of Motorcylce Maintenance by Robert Pirsig (1974)) and the new (e.g., Chicken Soup for the Soul by Mark Hansen and Jack Canfield (1993) or Tuesdays with Morrie by Mitch Albom (1997)) books that they hope will provide life-connecting experiences. More often than not, I have found most New Age approaches to serenity, peace, and fulfillment to be sappy, syrupy, and less than complete. The main character in the Zen of Motorcycle Maintenance seemed arrogant, at best, and as for Morrie, well, he encouraged people to follow their dreams, which may be a good thing, but I'm not sure that he remembered to mention that one person's dream touches the dreams of others. We need to consider our children, partner, relatives, friends, and neighbors.

I wonder if my colleague who thought she knew what I was thinking would have guessed that I am both open to and critical of most New Age spiritual material. She is aware that I am a critical scholar who attempts to combine creativity with critical thinking. It is the critical thinking that makes me question the benefits and the creativity that allows me to experience these things with open arms. However, I have been academically inclined to use critical theory in order to explore the political side of issues. In this case, whenever I am asked to consider writing a chapter, or developing a workshop on spirituality, I am immediately suspect about the intentions and the implications. In this case, I worry about the commodification and commercialization of spirituality. Like the concept of generosity as portrayed through St. Nick, which has been commercialized and commodified into a buying frenzy, I would hate to see spirituality publicized, commodified, commercialized, and eventually coca-cola-ized.

So I ask myself, why was I asked to contribute a chapter to this volume? Perhaps, it is because of my mixed ancestry. Perhaps, it is because I am not afraid to say what I dream, literally. For example, I wrote about how my grandmother visited me twice in my dreams while I was working on a book about her life (Clair, in progress).[2] When I told one person about this, he responded by saying, "That's odd. I thought Native Americans were supposed to have animals for their spirit guides."

Geez, I thought to myself, *I did not know she was my spirit guide. I just thought she was my grandmother. So here I am of Native heritage and I guess I did it wrong. Oh, well.*

On the other hand, maybe I am asked to conduct workshops or to write chapters on spirituality because I have written on phenomenology and the aesthetic approach to understanding our lives as creations (see Clair, 1998). Without a doubt, I believe that there is a connection between spirituality and aesthetics. Certainly, creative expression or the expression of creativity grounds the ephemeral. Ritual gives substance to religion, hymns give voice to an abstract joy, and Maharishi University gives place to the transcendental. From Michelangelo's *Pieta*, which provides an awe-inspiring expression of human sorrow and divine ecstasy, to the wisps of white sage and tobacco smoke sent swirling toward the clouds as an offering of the Original People's prayers, spirituality takes physical form through creativity.

On the other hand, as simple as it may sound, it is possible that I was asked to write this chapter because I tell a pretty good story, as well as study stories. And stories are at the heart and soul of the human spirit.

A goal of this book is to bring together essays that reflect on how spirituality may impact communication theory. I have devoted much of my scholarly career to exploring narrative theory and I do believe that spirituality may contribute to its refinement. So despite my reservations, in the following pages, I will lay the groundwork for how spirituality may indeed impact communication theory. Specifically, I will explore Native American spirituality and narrative theory.

Narrative Theory

In brief, narrative theory grew out of a rhetorical and philosophical school of thought that highlighted what is called the "linguistic turn." Nietzsche (1872/1954, 1873/1989, 1888/1974, 1901/1968), for example, argues that reality is a creation and we are the artists. Heidegger

(1926/1962) suggests that our very being relied on language. Language, everyday language, structures our world and only *interpretation* allows us to see what we have created. Heidegger's work reveals that language is the house of being and that we dwell in the word.

By the 1980s,[3] both rhetoricians and philosophers posed the idea that narratives act as the means to create and sustain communities (White, 1980; Fisher, 1984) or resist and challenge the social order (de Certeau, 1984). White (1980) for example, suggested that "to raise the question of the nature of narrative is to invite reflection on the very nature of culture and, possibly, even on the nature of humanity itself" (p. 5). Fisher, a rhetorician, added that human beings are *homo narrans*. That is to say, the very essence of being human is grounded in the ability to tell stories. Shared stories create community. But not all communities are prefaced on idyllic conditions. Colonization, for example, more often than not, resulted in the destruction and silencing of the stories of conquered people. In turn, these conquered people turned to whatever means available to save their stories. Sometimes their strategies of resistance included altering their stories to fit within the dominant group's story (de Certeau, 1984).

Less dramatic tales of oppression exist within cultures as well. Class, race, and gender have been determinants in the relative freedom to voice stories. Mumby (1987) addresses the political nature of narratives as he explores how the dominant group uses stories to control the subordinate group. In this particular case, Mumby studied a story regularly told to new employees at IBM. The story reinforces the hierarchal order of the organization and especially the taken-for-granted power invested in the CEO. Clair (1993) studied narratives that are not commonly shared in a community, but are instead whispered among a few. Specifically, Clair investigated the sequestered stories of sexual harassment. Helmer (1993) studied the dialectical tensions that are produced by organizational narratives. He focused his investigation on storytelling at a racetrack and unveiled the ways in which stories positioned people in terms of class, gender, and ethics.

Paul Ricoeur contributed additional insights to narrative theory. Drawing on the work of Heidegger, Ricoeur (1980) advances the notion of narrative time. Using the plot as his point of departure, he argues that narrative plot, as a series of events, provides an illusion of linear temporality. A deeper look into plot reveals that time unfolds in a dialectical fashion leading to an ending that begs a return to the beginning and one that simultaneously claims a sense of "now" while claiming a position in history. The beginning must contain the ending and the ending must contain the beginning if the narrative is to make sense. Thus, there exists a repetition within the narrative and a paradox of sorts.

Martin, Feldman, Hatch, and Sitkin (1983) explore the paradox of narrative at two levels. First, they study the internal paradoxes of organizational narratives. That is to say, they look at how narratives struggle with dialectical issues such as equality and inequality in organizational life. Second, they explore the idea that organizational stories are intended to be unique, to set one organization apart from another; and yet, organizational stories can be readily categorized into similar genres or types across organizations. Clair (1994) also demonstrates the simultaneous and paradoxical aspects of narrative as she interprets one man's story of sexual harassment and finds irony at multiple levels. Continuing the idea that narratives are saturated with paradox, Meyer (1997) explores humor in narrative and argues that humor is achieved through violation of normal patterns. Furthermore, humorous narratives in one organization served to "maintain unity in the face of diversity" (p. 188).

On a slightly different note, but still related to the sequential and self-contained aspects of narrative, Boje (1991) explored how stories are told and to whom within organizations. He notes that stories are not always necessarily the self-contained and structured linguistic event (i.e., beginning, middle, climax, and end) that is portrayed in most past scholarly writing. Instead, Boje discovered that stories are dynamic interrupt-able exchanges. They are frequently challenged, altered, and changed to meet the needs of the individual or the institution.

Taking an alternative approach to the study of narrative, Brown and McMillan (1991) argue that individual organizational stories can be collected to create a master text of an organization which can both reflect and represent the organization. The sub-texts can dialogue in such a way as to provide a master text or narrative to be further analyzed.

On a more pragmatic and pedagogical note, Clair, Chapman, and Kunkel (1996) argue that different forms of narrative act as pedagogical tools. They mention and describe personal narratives, case studies, interactive or collective narratives. They suggest that studying narrative pedagogy can contribute to the advancement of narrative theory. Specifically the authors argue that "narrative pedagogy is embedded with political, economic, and aesthetic undertones" (p. 254). Politically, narrative choice, structure, plot, audience and other related characteristics are subject to aspects of privilege. Economically, the narrative is produced for consumption although the audience does not always "buy the story" (p. 255). Aesthetically, the teller and listener are consumed by the emotional and artistic elements of the story. They are "infected" (Tolstoy, 1960) or "seduced" (Baudrillard, 1988) "by the narrative and possibly moved to personal or political action" (Clair, et al., 1996, p. 255).

Thus, numerous scholars have worked to advance, refine, and ameliorate narrative theory. In a continuing effort to add one more layer to narrative theory, I propose that spirituality may provide insights not yet considered.

Spirituality and Narrative Theory

It is beyond the scope of this chapter to provide the vast array of conceptualizations of spirituality. Mitroff and Denton (1999, as cited in Dehler & Neal, 2000) suggest that common threads exist between the multiple and varied definitions of spirituality. They list the following commonalities:

1. In contrast to conventional religion, spirituality is not formal, structured, or organized.
2. Spirituality is not denominational.
3. Spirituality is broadly inclusive; it embraces everyone.
4. Spirituality is universal and timeless.
5. Spirituality is the ultimate source and provider of meaning and purpose in our lives.
6. Spirituality expresses the awe we feel in the presence of the transcendent.
7. Spirituality is the sacredness of everything, including the ordinariness of everyday life.
8. Spirituality is the deep feeling of the interconnectedness of everything.
9. Spirituality is integrally connected to inner peace and calm.
10. Spirituality provides one with an inexhaustible source of faith and willpower.
11. Spirituality and faith are inseparable (see Mitroff & Denton, 1999, pp. 23-25 and Dehler & Neal, 2000, p. 537).

Obviously, discussions of what constitutes spirituality could fill volumes. Rather than confine my discussion to any one definition of spirituality, I will take up the *spirit* of the above list. Furthermore, for the purposes of this chapter, I will share three examples of how scholarly work in spirituality can contribute to communication theory, specifically narrative theory. First, I will address Karen Harlos' (2000) interpretive analysis of *Into Thin Air* (Krakauer, 1997), which relies on "spirituality" as an analytic and pedagogical tool. Second, I will discuss the contributions of Maria Christina Gonzalez (2000). Her work, which is entitled, *Seasons of Ethnography: A Creation-Centered Ontology for Ethnography*, may be applied to narrative theory. Finally, I will discuss my own recent work, which is entitled *Organizing Silence: A World of Possibilities,* on the aesthetic perspective, which includes a Native American aesthetic or spirituality. It too may provide a means of contributing to narrative theory.

Into Thin Air

Harlos (2000) designed a course for undergraduate students to explore how spirituality might advance their knowledge of organizational behavior. One of several assignment options included writing a critique of Krakauer's (1997) book, *Into Thin Air*. Harlos hoped to assess whether students would pick up on the possibilities of spirituality as an analytical tool for understanding the organizational, leadership, and decision-making behavior portrayed in the book. For example, Harlos explains that Krakauer includes descriptions of the tensions between "Eastern climbers--Tibetan Buddhist guides and Sherpas who carry not only supplies but sometimes clients themselves – and Western climbers, which include the two team leaders; other guides, and clients from Russia, the United States and New Zealand" (p. 622).

The Eastern climbers relate to the mountain as a sacred entity and refer to the mountain as "Chomolongma" ("goddess of the mountain"). When climbers begin their ascent they are entering "the house of the goddess" (Harlos, 2000, p. 622). The climb is approached with reverence. Prayers are said and the ascent to the top of the mountain and one's safe return are considered a collaborative effort between climbers and the Divine (Harlos, 2000).

The Western climbers relate to the mountain as if it is an inanimate object to be conquered. Ascent to the top is considered a commendable feat worthy of self-praise. God was invoked by westerners only under extreme duress as in the case of an American climber who cried again and again, "God, please let me live" as the descent turned into a nightmare (Harlos, 2000).

Harlos (2000) proposes that spirituality can help to explain decision-making, leadership, and organization as it is portrayed in the story, especially in light of the two different approaches to spirituality. The narrative becomes the site for spiritual reflection that then can be related to other situations in life. One of Harlos' students suggested that using spirituality with narrative allowed her "to answer questions she didn't know she wanted to ask" (p. 623).

Even when spirituality is not as obviously a part of a narrative as in the case of *Into Thin Air*, spirituality may be a means of raising questions about narrative that we have not asked before. Harlos suggests, for example, that questions of ethics and hard-core capitalism come under a different light when we apply spirituality to our critiques.

Seasons of Ethnography

Maria Christina Gonzalez (2000) lays out the ontology of a creation-centered form of ethnography under the title, *Seasons of Ethnography*. Her work is replete with spiritual guidance for ethnographers. She embraces Native American spirituality as a way to approach the study of culture as well as the study of self. According to Gonzalez, in order to develop *tentative* theories about another culture, a researcher must realize that they will come to know the culture in a *circular order, rhythmically*. The seasons act as a metaphorical guide for ethnographers as they *circle* and *spiral* forward with each stage or season of the ethnography proceeding in accordance with our time.

First, Gonzalez (2000) suggests that the *received view* is filled with assumptions that are taken-for-granted and which the researcher must be aware of in order to assess his/her own biases. These include: opportunism, independence of researcher, entitlement, and primacy of rationality. Once aware of these biases, a researcher may be better able to understand the guiding points of a Native American spiritual approach to ethnography. These guiding points include: an appreciation of natural cycles, interdependence of all things, preparedness, harmony and balance. If one moves into the field of study as fully prepared as possible and with respect, which includes respecting the interdependence of life forces, and respecting the dual contributions of rationality and emotionality, physicality and spirituality, then harmony and balance will follow.

Although Gonzalez' (2000) work is intended to guide ethnographers in ontological, epistemological, and methodological ways, I believe that this work can contribute substantially to our understanding and development of narrative theory, as well. But before I pursue this proposition, allow me to describe yet one more scholarly contribution.

Organizing Silence

In the book, *Organizing Silence*, Clair[4] (1998) promotes an aesthetic perspective as a guide for developing "communication theory" (p. 186). She sees the aesthetic perspective as "philosophical, political, phenomenological, and spiritual" (p. 186). Philosophically and politically, the author draws from critical, feminist, and postmodern theories. Phenomenologically, the author discusses Heidegger and others. Spiritually, the author draws from Awiakta's writing and her own Cherokee heritage.

The Cherokee philosophy of aesthetics suggests that aesthetics is woven into every aspect of life and is inseparable from all creation...patterns and rhythms sustain the heartbeat of humanity. A circular culture, rather than a linear one, that views life itself as an artistic creation. (p. 183)

The interconnectedness of all of life suggests that the world cannot be divided into components. Furthermore, "Harmony and balance are central to the Cherokee habits of being. Understanding simultaneous opposites as dwelling together creates an aesthetic that allows the Cherokee" (p. 183) to live a life of connection. This is what Awiakta (1993) refers to as the ability to "inhabit all its parts simultaneously" (p. 176) without privileging one view over another, which allows one to move from "intellect to the intuitive and back again (p. 177). Awiakta suggests that the Great Law celebrates "transitoriness" which is balanced with "continuance. . . .This is the Great Law, the Poem ensouled in the universe. The people sing it, dance it, live it" (p. 178). Clair (1998) suggests that:

> Cherokee aesthetics, like most Native American aesthetics, wraps the universe around our shoulders like a beautiful blanket or a delicate shawl. Surrounded by all of the creations and recognizing their connections allows one to listen to the silence . . . (p. 184)

Listening to the silence leads one to respectful expression.

Expression comes in many forms and is woven throughout daily life, which captures the essence of the universe. Aesthetics and communication are intricately woven together for the Cherokee who believe that reality is a rich interpretive process (Clair, 1998, p. 184).

Clair (1998) suggests that an aesthetic perspective encourages researchers to search for hidden ironies, expose the silenced within the silenced, look for realities that are woven within realities, and recognize themselves as artists in the creation of the interpretation (see p. 194). Clair's aesthetic perspective, like Gonzalez' creation-centered perspective, has not been specifically linked to narrative theory. Yet, these perspectives on spirituality and aesthetics could contribute to narrative theory in several ways.

Narrative theorists might expand their insights by viewing narratives as interconnected. For example, Mumby's (1987) study of the story told at IBM which he interprets to be a political tool of oppression might be studied further in relation to the responding narratives. For example, what narratives follow the telling of the IBM story? Are there narratives of resistance or hegemony? Are there humorous narratives, sarcastic narratives, challenging narratives, supportive narratives that are connected to the initial narrative? Interconnectedness would shed light on the fact that stories do not stand alone.

Narrative theory might also benefit from including the Native American notion that experiences occur in cyclic patterns. For example, Clair's (1996) study of the stories that college students told about their experiences with what constitutes *a real job* could be revisited during cyclic changes in the economy or across generations to better understand how stories reflect and create or, at the very least, contribute to socio-economic conditions as they are expressed through the grand narratives (i.e., capitalism). Cycles might be apparent in individuals' stories as they circle and spiral over the years. A value that surfaces in early stories may return later in life. Furthermore, stories might go through seasonal cycles of their own. For example, the seeds of a story might develop, be shared and later put to rest. Scholars might also explore how narratives nourish us, excite us, calm us, and let us rest.

The Native American perspective suggests that artificial boundaries cannot be sustained if we want to see how the world works. Stories that are deemed organizational stories are, most likely, carried home and shared with family members. How these stories and the responses that surround them contribute to understanding not only both life worlds, but also the artificial division that has been constructed around them, between them, should be of interest to scholars, especially those who study the corporate colonization of all life worlds (e.g., see Deetz, 1992).

Both Clair (1998) and Gonzalez (2000) draw upon "creation" to describe how words develop into realities. Gonzalez draws on nature's form of creation and Clair draws on the aesthetic creation. Creation, as a part of nature, grounds us as connected to Mother Earth; and, creation, as an artistic endeavor, lets us soar among the stars and revel in the universe--

Mother Earth and Sister Sun. The stories that sustain cultures that both ground them and speak of their creative developments and change may help us to recognize that stories are no more static than people or cultures. Narratives breathe life into a culture.

Narrative theory may well be advanced, refined, or altered in some way by exploring spiritual stories or by exploring stories in a spiritual way. Seasons, rhythmic cycles, interdependence, respect, and the simultaneity of existence are guiding principles that might enlighten our understanding of narrative. For example, if we call upon the Native American idea that all parts can be inhabited simultaneously, which is similar to Riceour's (1980) philosophy of narrative time, then we might see that the beginning contains the ending. Perhaps, the beginning of my chapter contains within it elements of the ending.

A Circular Ending

"Words are sacred . . . Words are spiritual . . .It is this spiritual force of words that enables them to create reality. It is also the reason behind the unwillingness of traditional native people to speak when they have nothing to say" (Gonzalez, 2000, p. 646). Words create our realities and the "spiritual force will come back to the sender" (Gonzalez, p. 646).

I was ever so hesitant to write or speak on the topic of spirituality, when my colleague and friend asked me to help put together a panel on work and spirituality. More than anything, I feared that I would be contributing to the commodification of the sacredness of life. Secondly, I feared being inundated with the sappy, syrupy, touchy-feely stuff that makes up "spirituality." Better for me to write on the topic of aesthetics, I thought. But spirituality leaked into my writings anyway. Ironically, it is a Native American spirituality that readily offers an explanation: Here, I suspect that Awiakta would remind me that spirituality and aesthetics inhabit each other. They embrace each other and wrap themselves around us through the words, the dances, the songs, and especially, the stories of life.

Notes:

1. Transcendental meditation has a long history. By calling it New Age I am merely referring to its introduction into the United States during the 1970's and its widely popularized benefits as alternative spirituality.

2. Clair, R.P. (in progress). *Echoes of a silence: A historical novel.* Portions of this novel have been presented at the annual meeting of the National Communication Association, Chicago – 1999 as part of the panel entitled "The Novel as Cultural Analysis."

3. A special issue of Critical Inquiry (1980) was devoted to the discussion of narrative theory. Contributors included Haydon White, Victor Turner, Jacques Derrida, Roy Schafer, Barbara Hernstein Smith and Ursula Le Guin to name a few.

4. While I may appear schizophrenic by switching from first person to third person to refer to my own scholarly work, I have done so for the reader's benefit. I have used third person to speak of my own solo work as well as my collaborative research in the literature review sections of this chapter and I switch to first person in the opening and closing commentaries.

References
Albom, M. (1997). *Tuesdays with Morrie: An old man, a young man, and life's greatest lessons.* New York: Doubleday.
Awiakta, M. (1993). *Selu: Seeking the Corn Mother's wisdom.* Golden, CO: Fulcrum.
Baudrillard, J. (1988). *The ecstacy of communication.* (B. Schutze & C. Schultz, Trans.; S. Lotringer, Ed.). New York: Semiotexte.
Boje, D.M. (1991). The storytelling organization: A study of story performance in an office-supply firm. *Administrative Science Quarterly, 36,* 106-126.
Brown, M.H., & McMillan, J.J. (1991). Culture as text: The development of an organizational narrative. *Southern Communication Journal, 57,* 49-60.
Clair, R.P. (1993). The use of framing devices to sequester organizational narratives: Hegemony and harassment. *Communication Monographs, 60,* 113-136.
Clair, R.P. (1994). Resistance and oppression as a self-contained opposite: An organizational communication analysis of one man's story of sexual harassment. *Western Journal of Communication, 58,* 235-262.
Clair, R.P. (1996). The political nature of the colloquialism, "a real job": Implications for organizational socialization. *Communication Monographs, 63,* 249-267.
Clair, R.P. (1998). *Organizing silence: A world of possibilities.* Albany, NY: State University of New York Press.
Clair, R.P., Chapman, P.A., & Kunkel, A.W. (1996). Narrative approaches to raising consciousness about sexual harassment: From research to pedagogy and back again. *Journal of Applied Communication research, 24,* 241-259.
Clair, R.P., & Kunkel, A.W. (1998). "Unrealistic realities": Child abuse and the aesthetic resolution. *Communication Monographs, 65,* 24-46.
de Certeau, M. (1984). *The practice of everyday life.* Berkeley: University of California Press.
Deetz, S. A. (1992). *Democracy in an age of corporate colonization: Developments in communication and the politics of everyday life.* Albany: State University of New York Press.
Dehler, G. & Neal, J. (2000). The guest editor's corner: Special issue, Spirituality in contemporary work: Its place, space, and role in management education. *Journal of Management Education, 24,* 536-539.
Fisher, W. (1984). Narration as a human communication paradigm:

The case of public moral argument. *Communication Monographs, 51*, 1-22.

Gabriel, Y. (1991). Turning facts into stories and stories into facts: A hermeneutic exploration of organizational folklore. *Human Relations, 44*, 857-875.

Gonzalez, M.C. (2000). The four seasons of ethnography: A creation-centered ontology for ethnography. *International Journal of Intercultural Relations, 24*, 623-650.

Hansen, M.V. & Canfield, J. (1993). *Chicken soup for the soul: 101 stories to open the heart and rekindle the spirit.* Deerfield Branch, FL: Health Communications.

Harlos, K.P. (2000). Toward a spiritual pedagogy: Meaning, practice, and applications in management education. *Journal of Management Education, 24*, 612-627.

Heidegger, M. (1962). *Being and time.* New York: Harper & Row. (Original work published 1926)

Helmer, J. (1993). Storytelling in the creation and maintenance of organizational tension and stratification. *Southern Communication Journal, 59*, 34-44.

Hesse, H. (1999). *Siddhartha.* (S. Appelbaum, Trans. & K. Casey, Ed.). (Original work published 1922)

Krakauer, J. (1997). *Into thin air: A personal account of the Mount Everest disaster.* New York: Villard.

Martin, J., Feldman, M.S., Hatch, M.J., & Sitkin, S.B. (1983). The uniqueness paradox in organizational stories. *Administrative Science Quarterly, 28*, 438-453.

Meyer, J.C. (1997). Humor in member narratives: Uniting and dividing at work. *Western Journal of Communication, 61*, 188-208.

Mitroff,I., & Denton, E. (1999). *A spiritual audit of corporate America: A hard look at spirituality, religion, and values in the workplace.* San Francisco: Josey-Bass.

Mumby, D.K. (1987). The political function of narrative in organizations. *Communication Monographs, 54*, 113-127.

Nietzsche, F. (1954). *The birth of tragedy from the spirit of music* (Trans. P. Fadiman). In *The Philosophy of Nietzsche* (pp. 947-1088). New York: Random House (Original work published 1872)

Nietzsche, F. (1968). *The will to power – 1870-1888* (Trans. W. Kaufmann & R.J. Hollingdale). New York and London: Vintage Books. (Original work published 1901)

Nietzsche, F. (1974). *The twilight of the idols.* In O. Levy (Ed.) &

A.M. Ludovici (Trans.), *The complete works of Friedrich Nietzsche.* New York: Gorden Press. (Original work published 1888)

Nietzsche, F. (1989). *On truth and lying in an extra-moral sense.* In S. Gilman, C. Blair, & D. Parent (Eds. & Trans.), *Friedrich Nietzsche on rhetoric and language.* New York: Oxford University Press. (Original work published 1873)

Persig, R.M. (1974). *Zen and the art of motorcycle maintenance.* Toronto and New York: Bantam.

Ricoeur, P. (1980). Narrative time. *Critical Inquiry, 7,* 169-190.

Tolstoy, L. (1960). *What is art?* (A. Maude, Trans.). Indianapolis, IN: Hackett. (Original work published 1896)

White, H. (1980). The value of narrativity in the representation of reality. *Critical Inquiry, 7,* 5-27.

Chapter 6

Faith in Each Other:
Encountering a Communicative Ethics

Natalie Lynn Sydorenko
Purdue University

Abstract

A central concern of communication teacher-scholars is being able to articulate a point of departure for a communicative ethics. Through my engagement with various theoretical and philosophical texts, and in conjunction with my lived experiences as a spiritual being, I argue for a communicative ethics grounded in my "radical roots," both academic and religious. I identify the role of human responsibility in the shaping of a communicative ethics as well as the function of narrative in both communication and ethics. Finally, I discuss some implications for a multi-disciplinary curriculum across the fields of communication, philosophy and the social sciences.

A Rhizomatic Beginning

In trying to provide a point of departure for a communicative ethics I find myself uncertain about how to begin. Believing that both philosophical and theological thinking inform an ethics of humane being-in-the-world, I am bereft of a particular foundation or single theory from which to proceed. Since the relationship between communication and ethics is both philosophical and spiritual, at least in my lived experience, the discourses that allow me to speak on this subject come from disparate pools of energy. As such, I will enter this narrative like a rhizome, with extended lines of flight. Gilles Deleuze and Felix Guattari's (1987) discursive strategy of the rhizome allows me access to places I might not know how to venture near otherwise. The rhizome, like my story here, has overlay and continuity. It is a form of minoritarian literature offering a voice in the larger dialogue. Minoritarian texts can demonstrate "repetition with difference." The multiple voices that speak in this narrative do the same. Deleuze and Guattari suggest, "Write, form a rhizome, increase your territory by deterritorialization, extend the line of flight to the point where it becomes an abstract machine covering the entire plane of consistency" (p. 11).

The questions surrounding communication and ethics are ones which imply *connections*. Note Deleuze and Guattari, "A rhizome ceaselessly establishes connections between semiotic chains, organizations of power, and circumstances relative to the arts, sciences, and social struggles" (p. 7). In trying to establish these connections, I must enter the narrative from many plateaus. Describing the rhizome in *A Thousand Plateaus: Capitalism and Schizophrenia*, Deleuze and Guattari propose that we need to understand books, rhetoric, music – all discourse – as fragmentary, interrelated texts, as performances that are not rooted and singular, but rather operate as lines of flight which are multiplicitous. "A plateau is always in the middle," they contend, "not at the beginning or the end. A rhizome is made of plateaus" (p. 21). Understanding self and society (communication and ethics), or, in other terms, "a dynamic becoming," involves the embracing of multiplicity over unity, flexibility over stability, and heterogeneity over homogeneity. And this becoming is constantly brought forth through ruptures. Ruptures are part of communication, and these ruptures in communication imply a constant overlaying of rhizomes.

My first rupture or line of flight takes me (though simultaneously with the others) to my personal basis for a communicative ethics. From this familiar yet ever-changing plateau, I immediately think of my mother and father. They taught me more than any text or lecture of what it means to speak of a *communicative ethics*. Since my earliest days I can remember my parents tending to their modest garden and the vibrant flowers that graced our yard. They cared for animals, our family, friends, and others around them with strength and compassion. They taught my brother and I to do the same. Growing up, I attended both my Mother's Polish National Catholic Church and my Father's Ukrainian Orthodox church. I tried to practice both faiths, as well as engage my Protestant schoolmates' theological ideas. Very truly, I believed that following Jesus Christ was the path to living ethically with other beings. But I am a curious sort, like a cat. Soon my college days found me immersed in texts rich with philosophies and understandings of the world that were dramatically *other* from my religious understandings of the world.

Years in academia have passed, and necessarily I have encountered various ways of understanding the nature of Being. Now, as a student on her way to crossing another threshold into selfhood by actualizing my space in the educational field, my temporal present negotiates my past and my future. I know that I am both a social and spiritual being. My learning about the social construction of the world does not preclude me from retaining my belief that I am a child of God, nor does it prohibit me from being able to apprehend the loving struggle of authentic communication. Rather, by embracing both the wavering nature of sociality and the overwhelming feeling of a "universal" energy that guides us, I am resigned to live in acknowledgment of a "convergence without coincidence" amongst my multiple lines of flight (see Schrag, 1997).

I remember thinking, when I was a small child, that the weight of the world was within me – longing and waiting to escape, to be free, to free others. Sometimes the sunlight still hits my face in a way that I know I am one with all the world. Other times, the shadows of politics and capitalism, individualism and success, cast a dark shroud upon me that I cannot seem to shake off. I feel lost and disconnected in my relations with others, and yet I know this is not truly so. It is only a seeming – a lack of intention, a disinterested intention, on the part of myself or the other. And I know that truly being real is being with others, wholly, fully – giving without expectation of return. To see God in the face of the Other and to feel humbled by her whole presence is living in the Spirit. *The Gift* of *Love*. This is the gift that I continue to believe Christ gave – one that bleeds us not dry of financial means, but one that asks nothing more than time and compassion. 'Tis a shame that such gifts are running low in the superstore of humanity. But I digress. Approaching now another plateau, I leave this one with a summative reflection: during my predominantly theist years, I could not have realized that my journey toward self-hood and being-with-others in the world was only beginning . . .

A Philosophical and Theological Basis for Communicative Ethics

Throughout the years spent in classrooms that rustled with a plurality of ontological and epistemological ideas, the words of various thinkers and scholars re-told my childhood lessons of how to be in the world with others, animals and nature and opened my mind to a much deeper appreciation of ethical living. Though spirituality largely shaped my understanding of and responsibility for a communicative ethics, I began to see the orientations of other theorists enhancing and illuminating the perspectives I held (and still hold). As a Master's student in Communication I was introduced to Joseph Campbell's world of myth. Drawn to his writings on both Eastern and Western religions, his work eventually guided my Master's thesis. For Campbell (1973), the point of departure for a communicative ethics lies in the individual's adventure of transcendence, a transcendence that leads her back into her community as a self-actualized, responsible citizen. Where we thought we were alone, we discover that we are one with all the world. In other words, an individual must reconcile him or herself to the mystery of the universe as it is, and then experience the revelation to waking consciousness of the "powers of its own sustaining source" (p. 5). The challenge of living the individual journey is only heightened by the fact that an individual must "heed the call" within the cultural body of his or her society. To Campbell, this is a critical and vital function of mythology. Myth functions: ". . . to foster the centering and unfolding of the individual in integrity, in accord with *d)* himself (the microcosm), *c)* his culture (the mesocosm), *b)* the universe (the macrocosm), and *a)* that awesome ultimate mystery which is both beyond and within himself and all things . . . (p. 6)

Campbell's visions of self-actualization as a way toward ethical consciousness, spawned greatly from Eastern philosophies, now greatly contributed to my understanding of a communicative ethics. Soon thereafter, my studies led me to a hearty engagement with the works of rhetorical theorist/critic Kenneth Burke. Burke's approach to communication and ethics quickly found purchase in the growing expanse of theories I embraced, which, while different, spoke in similar registers. Burke (1984), in discussing *orientation* (toward the world), suggests that an orientation "moves to form a closed circle, though individual or class divergencies ever tend to break the regularity of this circle." "Essentially, however, we [aim] to show that the circle is basically *ethical*" (p. 262). He goes on to purport that although he does not agree with Lawrence's "ethical universe-building," "we contend that there is no other kind of orientation possible" (p. 263). In Burkean terms, then, this means that as symbol-using animals we are naturally oriented toward ethical symbolic actions, actions motivated by our ability to use language.

Furthermore, throughout his work, Burke asserts a relationship between love and the act of communication. In his text *Language as Symbolic Action* (1966), he exclaims: "'Love' names an ideal, desired state of communion that, as technically attenuated, amounts to 'communication'" (p. 377). As well, despite his agnostic position, Burke (1970) dedicates an entire book to a study in logology via *The Rhetoric of Religion* (title and subject). Interpreting Western Christianity, he explains that if theology is the study of The Word (words about God), then logology is the study of "words about words," establishing an analogy between the two. He suggests that, perhaps, our *purpose* as word-people is to act in accord with the Upward Way. Christianity and language intimate such a purpose:

> Linguistically, [then,] the analogue of the Trinity would be: 'Father' equals the thing named (*esse*): 'Son' equals the name (*nosse*, Christ as "the Word"); 'Holy Spirit' equals the perfect concordance or communion between named and name (*velle*), a relations of conformity that is properly expressed, from the personal point of view, as love (p. 377).

Along with my growing affinity for Burke and his orientation toward communication and ethics, other voices would soon ask me to engage them. While still searching for answers or reasons for establishing a communicative ethics, I encountered phenomenological Continental thought. My introduction to the philosophies of Edmund Husserl and Martin Heidegger led me to contemplate, to a much greater extent than ever before, the question of what it means to *be* in the world as a *Being*. For Husserl, we, as beings, experience life from the world of the natural standpoint, where our concrete senses apprehend that which shows itself and is directly presented, including its value characteristics. Husserl (1931, see works cited for complete citation) explains: "this world is not there for me as a mere *world of facts and affairs*, but, with the same immediacy, as a *world of values*, a *world of goods*, a *practical world*" (p. 70). He further asserts that when we experience a phenomenon, "the objective element does not only meet one's gaze as "itself" in general, and we are not only aware of it as 'given,' but it confronts us as a self given *in its purity, wholly and entirely as it is in itself"* (p.106). Being, then, is an object for a subject (of consciousness) and made known to us through a synthesis of the presentative acts of consciousness in conjunction with the presentative profiles of the object-as-meant. The transcendental conditions of conscious-Being provide us with the ability to bracket the object as it presents itself to us in its full essence in our perception, imagination and conception. From the transcendental standpoint, we can experience a particular exhibiting a universal. For me, such a notion resonated with Campbell's perspective, though each man arrived at his understanding of the experience of being by way of a different path.

But this type of transcendental phenomenological idealism operates according to the tenents of modernity. Husserl's theory retains the elements of idealism insofar as each particular experience of consciousness directly corresponds to a pre-determined truth that we need only uncover in order to understand the nature of Being and universal essence. Consequently, since I believed (and still do) myself to be a feminist scholar of communication, Husserl's project could only contribute to my larger understanding of self and other relations, but could not alone serve as a point of departure for ethical comportment toward living beings. Moreover, I was not convinced that seeking the truth from phenomena was the definitive motivation for a communicative ethics.

Heidegger, advancing the thought of Husserl, provided me with more extensions of and lines of flight toward an understanding of *being* through his conception of Dasein. Heidegger (1993) explains: "This being which we ourselves in each case are and which includes inquiry among the possibilities of its Being we formulate terminologically as *Dasein*" (p. 47-8). Heidegger extends Husserl's theory with the interpretation of everyday concrete experiences in a categorical sense and not in a manner which raises the question of ontology. This "ontic-ontological priority of Dasein is therefore the reason why the specific constitution of the Being of Dasein – understood in the sense of the "categorical" structure that belongs to it – remains hidden from it" (p. 58). In other words, our daily concrete engagement with the world while being-in-the-world obscures from our view the ontological existentials of our universal structure; and, yet, it is the ontic dimension of Dasein that affords us the opportunity to posit the question of what it means *to be*. "Dasein is ontically 'closest' to itself, while ontologically farthest away; but pre-ontologically it is surely not foreign to itself" (p. 58). It is only through the ontic (beings-entities, categories, concrete everyday experience) that we may know the ontological (Being, extistentials, the universal structure of life).

An interpretation of Dasein is only possible with a view toward temporality and the "explication of time as the transcendental horizon [with its limitless possibilities or potentials for *being*] of the question of Being" (p. 87). "Time," which Heidegger suggests serves the ontological but swiftly retracts and connects it with the ontic, is a necessary condition for the contextual understanding of Dasein as Being-in-the-World (p. 61). As "temporal" beings, we experience Truth as disclosure and Being as historical presence (i.e. "natural processes and historical events are separated from . . . spatial and numerical relationships"). When we remember that we are "always already there," we experience Dasein-as-Being-in-the-World.

In other words, when Dasein discovers itself, it discovers this premise ("always already there"). Dasein is characterized by "being thrown" into the world without prior consultation. There is a pre-theoretical attunement to the world that we can interpret by our being involved in the world through our particular projects. Moreover, this Being-in-the-World is articulated through language. Since the meaning of Dasein is temporality, it contains the co-dependent determinants of past, present and future. Within the basic structure of Dasein (whose task it is to discover its ontological existential), we find situationality and facticity--the past, and understanding (projective) – the future.

Language, which is of the present, functions to articulate the dimensions of temporality and understanding (past, present and future). It is through language (one of the constitutive features of Dasein) that we can achieve contextual understanding, with "Being as historical (temporal) presence" and intentionality (of Dasein) as a mode of existence. "All research [or communicative action] . . . is an ontic possibility of Dasein. The Being of Dasein finds its meaning in temporality. . . . This understanding discloses the possibilities of its Being and regulates them" (p. 63). Yet for Heidegger, the schemata of the ego-cogita-cogitata triad is replaced by the situatedness of a *being* in time and space which reveals the neutrality of what it means *to be*. Here is where I must depart from Heidegger's ontology in that I cannot reconcile temporality and historicity as neutral with regard to *being*. The "dominant" culture "restores" time through health care, satisfying basic needs and luxury wants, education, leisure, etc. History and temporality are not "neutrally" experienced by all individuals. Yet, if we "use all that is there to use" as Burke advises, or simply view the phrase which I now cannot separate from Heidegger, *being-in-the-world-with-others*, as suggestive of how we should encounter the Other, we can move into greater understanding of wholeness in a communicative ethics. From Heidegger's basic standpoint, then, much like Burke's, language is the point of departure for a communicative ethics.

So too for Martin Buber. Only recently has the work of Martin Buber come into my experience and my world of relations. His conviction toward language for its ability to communicate relation is as bold as that of Burke or Heidegger. He asserts:

> And just as talk in a language may well first take the form of words in the brain of the man, and then sound in his throat, and yet both are merely refractions of the true event, for in actuality speech does not abide in man, but man takes his stand in speech and talks from there; so with every word and every spirit. Spirit is not in the I, but between I and Thou. (1958, p. 63)

And much like Heidegger, Buber interprets Being as twofold. He asserts that for (wo)man, the world is twofold, in accordance with her/his twofold attitude. These two *folds* represent the primary words that humans speak: *I-Thou* and *I-It*. Only when we speak the *Thou* are we able to enter into relation with another *Thou* in her or his whole presence. Though we cannot live without the world of *I-It*, there is no real living without the speaking the *Thou* from our whole being. As Buber believes, "All real living is meeting" (p.11). From this necessarily dialogic approach to being and communication, it is the *other* who, in relation, forms the basis for a communicative ethics. He observes, "The relation with man is the real simile of the relation with God; in it true address receives true response; except that in God's response everything, the universe, is made manifest as language" (p. 103). Buber's perspective, though coming from a foundation in Judaism, has been the perspective thus far in my academic studies that resonates most with my spiritual understanding of The Gift, Christ's agape love, and the compassion of Buddha.

Though I mourn the restrictions of "time" upon my ability to study everyone and everything I would like to learn, what I have encountered thus far in my lived experience and in my pursuit of a communicative ethics has allowed me to create a mapping by which to connect various thinkers who, despite their different tongues, speak in the languages of a civic humanity. For example, I am not intimately familiar with the works of Soren Kierkegaard or Emmanuel Levinas, as most likely I should be. However, by encountering them through the writings and teachings of Calvin O. Schrag, I am able to discern how these orientations toward a communicative ethics also converge with the lines of flight in my narrative. Schrag (1997) explains that there are lines of convergence between Kierkegaard's Christian consciousness and Levinas's Jewish consciouness. "When Levinas speaks of love as a transcendence that reaches to the Other and then reverberates back to the side of immanence, his words could be attributed to Kierkegaard as well" (p.146). Schrag further explains that *both* Western and Eastern literatures of religion have their own "stories to tell about the ways of transcendence as exemplified in the works of love . . . [and about] transcendence as gift-giving."

I am suggesting that there are lines of convergence among all of the voices re-presented in this narrative. These different yet similar influences weave themselves together in my consciousness, like a kind of "cross-reading," echoing Schrag's own words about Kierkegaard and Levinas: "Such a cross-reading would not only uncover some remarkable similarities between representatives of different religions, but it would also nurture a transversal communication that struggles to maintain itself across often-diverging viewpoints" (p. 146). Theses *voice lines* converge and thus present a point of departure for a communicative ethics which radiates transversally within our humanity, is experienced through language, and en*act*ed for the purposes of love and transcendence.

Community and Responsibility

Entering here the plateau of community and responsibility, or, what we might call a *communal responsibility toward beings-in-the-world,* intertextual lines of flight connect to the "convergent" point(s) of departure described above. All of the perspectives presented thus far in my narrative address the role of responsibility in the shaping of a communicative ethic. Here, the term *responsibility* implies ethical action toward self, other and the community at large. It is this notion of a responsibility to *be* human, and, as such, to care for others, that enables us to create a civic, ethical discourse from which to proceed. We might consider such a notion, in tandem, with Schrag's (1997) description of the self in community in *The Self after Postmodernity.* As well, his discussion of Heidegger illuminates the role of responsibility with regard to *other*:

> One of the more significant moments in the scenario of the call of conscience as portrayed by Heidegger is the recognition that heeding the call is both an individual task and a social responsibility in which the individuated *Dasein* faces the other, and it faces the other *either* in the unauthentic mode of conventionalism, mass hysteria, and the superimposition of ideality, *or* in the authentic mode of creative intersubjective self-actualization. (p. 95)

This identification of two modes by which we might engage the other resonates with Buber's (1958) distinction between addressing the other as *I-It* or as *I-Thou*. He exclaims: "How powerful is the unbroken world of *It*, and how delicate are the appearances of the *Thou*!" (p. 98, original emphasis). As well, both of these viewpoints may be likened to M. M. Bakhtin's discussion of addressivity and answerability (see *Toward a Philosophy of the Act* and *Art and Answerability)* as well as Campbell's "call to the mystery." All three favor and encourage this authentic mode (of self/other relations).

Buber (1958) speaks of the Spirit, like many others I have been told about through conversations with my peers on the subject of *giving* but have yet to engage through reading. For Buber, Spirit becomes word, arising from "this world's meetings with the other." "He who knows the breadth of the Spirit trespasses if he desires to get power over the Spirit or to ascertain its nature and qualities. But he is also disloyal when he ascribes the gift to himself" (pp. 129-30). Living in the Spirit means we "cannot approach others with what we have received, and say 'You must know this, you must do this.' We can only go, and confirm its truth. . . . we *must*" (p. 111, original emphasis). The living word appears, for Buber, when the solidarity of connection between *I* and the world is renewed. This happens when we give to the other of our whole being and wholly embrace hers.

Similarly, Bakhtin believes that (a Buberian) *I* enters into language, and, in doing so, dwells ethically in the world. As Holoquist explains: "For Bakhtin, the unity of an act [of speech] and its account, a deed and its meaning . . . is never a priori, but which must always and everywhere be achieved" (1993, p. xii, as appears in the foreword to Bakhtin's *Toward a Philosophy of the Act*). The actually performed *act*, "somehow knows, somehow possesses the unitary and once-occurrent being of life," Bakhtin says. "It orients itself within that being, and it does so, moreover, in its entirety – both in its content aspect and in its actual, unique factuality" (p. 28). There is no alibi in existence for Bakhtin. Only in the unity of our answerability for every once-occurent moment (or utterance) do we take a stand in the word. We respond. "Responsibility, then," explains Holoquist (19, "is the ground of moral action, the way in which we overcome the guilt of the gap between our words and deeds, even though we do not have an alibi in existence" (p. xiii). Says Bakhtin, "It is only my non-alibi in being that transforms an empty possibility into an actual answerable act or deed" (1993, p.42).

The articulations of a communicative ethics up to this point, at least to me, seem ideal. They echo the lessons I learned in Sunday school and the vividly painted faces of God in my devoutly iconic Orthodox church. Sitting in the pew I was certain God could see me, hear me, listen to my mind's thoughts. It was such a penetrating *gaze*, but I felt safe surrounded by it. Unfortunately, not all gazes are experienced in that way. I am proceeding along these lines (of flight) in order to identify one of the main ways this communicative, ethical "ideal" is abandoned in community. The *gaze* can be oppressive and, borrowing from Schrag, even "life-negating." He asserts, "The 'sociality' of being-with is always already oriented either toward a creative and life-affirming intersubjectivity or toward a destructive and life-negating mode of being-with-others" (1997, p. 88). Ethical responsibility of self toward other and community is lost. Through his discussion of Dewey's sense of community, Schrag explains that a "community" is not fashioned on technology nor is it a "value-free description of a societal state of affairs." A communal being-with-others implies normative, evaluative signifiers.

In fact, communities are made, in part, of power-relations. Through Foucault's (1995) interpretation of the Panopticon, power relations are seen as transferring from an institutionalized state of control to an individualized state of control. For those who wish to remain at the top of the hierarchical structure of a society, this type of control becomes an extremely efficient and self-regulatory process for maintaining power relations. The Panopticon, because of its totalizing effect, was designed to foster self-discipline. In other words, the surveillance allows for control, a control which leads to the reform of a criminal, and, ultimately, of all people in a society. Through the panoptic system, a transformation occurs. Prisoners (read here also: *citizens*), newly regenerated through internalized power relations, can re-enter society as "generally free" individuals with the capacity to self-monitor their actions. Consequently, power becomes and is pervasive through a ritualized, institutionalized, and, ultimately, internalized form of discipline and control.

We must move away from surveillance toward responsibility. Away from "discipline and control" and toward ethical, communal acts of responsibility toward others. As beings-in-the-world we are ethically responsible for being-in-the-world with others, with animals, with nature. But the messages of the Panopticon (i.e. power, control, supervision, self-discipline) are present without the structure. They are embedded into society, and as such, they are less a concrete form of every morality than they "are a set of physico-political techniques" (p. 223). Foucault explains:

> There is no risk, therefore, that the increase of power created by the panoptic machine may degenerate into tyranny; the disciplinary mechanism will be democratically controlled, since it will be constantly accessible 'to the great tribunal committee of the world.' This Panopticon, subtly arranged so that an observer may observe, at a glance, so many different individuals, also enables everyone to come and observe any of the observers. The seeing machine was once a sort of dark room into which individuals spied; it has become a transparent building in which the exercise of power may be supervised by society as a whole. (p. 207)

The "great tribunal committee of the world" can still exist – holding self and other responsible for ethical comportment toward one another without the dehumanization of the Panoptic machine.

Cultural and societal boundaries do not divide us as a human race nor as extensions of the Absolute. Hegemonic rules serve only to disconnect, create isolation, and enhance the Panoptic effect. Osbon (1991), in a book dedicated to the visions of Joseph Campbell, explains that separating and segregating ourselves from our own society and from other cultures, is to "set oneself against wholeness" (p. 37). "To separate ourselves from the whole is to cut our options and erect the walls of our own prison," she states. What humans need to remember is that we are all connected by language and action. Schrag (1997) points out that the "characterization of the ethical as being composed of fitting responses within the context of community has been designed to call attention to ethics as a praxis . . ." (p. 101). "The ethical has to do with *ethos* in its orginative sense of a cultural dwelling," Schrag continues, "a mode or manner of historical existence, a way of being in the world that exhibits a responsibility both to oneself and to others." How we come to understand such responsibility is dependent upon our communicative acts with others. With that said, we move to the narrative plateau.

Connection through Narrative

Along with the nurturing and expressive actions of my family and friends, I have personally learned about the role of responsibility in canvassing a communicative ethics by embracing narrative life. From the eighth grade until I entered my Master's program I was inclined toward a life in literature and poetics. I was taken in rapture by the power of the narrative – in fiction, in conversation, in writing. I perceived my formal study of communication as only a "back up" to my real passion. Now, I could not imagine having taken another path. I have found a space to engage the other wherein matters such as communication, ethics and love might be taken up in earnest with commitment and connection. The communication discipline, by employing a plurality of "academic" narratives (e.g. philosophical, sociological, literary, cultural), provides "a thousand plateaus" by which I may study the human condition (but here I anticipate the next plateau of this rhizome). Getting back to the point, the function of narrative in both communication and ethics has been illuminated and stressed time and again.

Schrag (1997) describes two senses of the narrative. The "weaker" and more conventional sense is conceived as a form and style of discourse, while the "stronger" sense of narrative is a "form and dynamics of the self as life-experiencing subject" (p. 42). So narrative, much like experience, is twofold. Narrative is both a lexical entry for poetics and is expressive of an ontological claim. It is this latter understanding of narrative that Schrag is concerned with. He explains:

> Narrative is not simply the telling of a story by the who of discourse, providing a binding textuality of past and future inscriptions; it is also the emplotment of a personal history through individual and institutional action. Narrative thus provides the proper context for the amalgam of discourse and action that informs and drives the economy of communicative praxis. (p. 43)

Carr (1986) insists too that a "narrative structure pervades everyday life as the form of our experiences and actions" (p. 73). Narrative, by providing the keys to metaphysical, epistemological and moral notions of personal identity, is concerned with the question of how to live one's life as a whole (a concerned shared by Buber) both practically and ethically. Arising from this perspective of narrative's connection to lived experience we find sanctuary not only in the narrative schemata that shapes our humanness, but also in the function of narrative to secure a space for local stories within community life.

As a communication scholar influenced by postmodern perspectives, I find Lyotard's text, *The Postmodern Condition*, to be one of the most salient discourses regarding the function of local narratives in both communication and ethics. For Lyotard (1991), the *modern* designates "any science that legitimates itself with reference to a metadiscourse of [philosophy] making an explicit appeal to some grand narrative" (p. xxiii). By sharp contrast, he defines the *postmodern* as "incredulity toward metanarratives." The *modern*, employs a language game of science, one of "proofs" legitimated through the rules of its own game. As such, science "has always been in conflict with narratives." The former, through its own criteria, dismisses the latter as false, as being unable to reveal any truth-value or produce *knowledge*. Yet, as Lyotard explains, even "proof" needs to be "proven," and "scientific knowledge cannot know and make known that it is the true knowledge without resorting to the other, narrative, kind of knowledge, which from its point of view is no knowledge at all" (p. 29).

The artist, writer, and even philosopher (of which Lyotard labels himself in his introduction) must deny accepted forms. They must refuse "the consensus of a taste which would make it possible to share collectively the nostalgia for the unattainable." In the modern, nostalgia for the unattainable is preserved through discourses and language games that communicate grand narratives (e.g. Hegel's dialectic of the Spirit, Majoritarian hermeneutics, Marxism). Such meta-narratives are unable to articulate persisting differences, multiplicity, nor the pragmatics of narrative knowing. Says Lyotard, "The grand narrative has lost its credibility, regardless of what mode of unification it uses, regardless of whether it is a speculative narrative or a narrative of emancipation" (p. 37). They cannot nor do they try to present the unpresentable.

These grand narratives signify what is *modern* in society. Lyotard continues, "The postmodern, [then], would be that which, in the modern, puts forward the unpresentable itself; that which denies itself the solace of good forms, the consensus of a taste which would make it possible to share collectively the nostalgia for the unattainable; that which searches for new presentations, not in order to enjoy them but in order to impart a stronger sense of the unpresentable" (p. 81). Localized narratives (which do search for new presentations), as opposed to a metanarrative, represent postmodernism as modernism in its "nascent state." Lyotard explains that Joyce allows the unpresentable to become perceptible in his writing itself, "A whole range of available narrative and even stylistic operators is put into play without concern for the unity of the whole, and new operators are tried" (p. 80). And yet, the potential for Joyce's work to communicate a *localized* narrative is compromised by its nostalgia for the unattainable (since his use of language appears as "rituals originating in piety . . . which prevent the unpresentable from being put forth"). The *post modern* – artist, writer, discourse – must work without rules in order to "formulate the rules of what *will have been done*." At least Joyce, through his experimenting with language in a broad and diverse way without a concern for a "unity of the whole," is not afraid to entertain the sublime. As Joseph Campbell (1988) has noted, "Joyce's trick was seeing symbols everywhere." And what did Joyce write about? The experience of humanity.

As Lyotard says of the state of affairs (of his time): "According to this version [the current condition of knowledge in the most highly developed societies], knowledge finds its validity not within itself, not in a subject that develops by actualizing its learning possibilities, but in a practical subject – humanity" (p. 35). We must call science out on its strategies to legitimate itself, and instead, embrace local narratives, create works of art or produce discourse that articulates humanity – the most practical and real subject we can know. Traditional science and its various discourses cannot address or account for the disparate, narrative experiences of life. Science must be revolutionary, it must also supply allusions to the conceivable that cannot be "legitimated" through scientific terms. But if modernity persists, the postmodern is inevitably there in its nascent state. And if we must depend on the aesthetic community to present the postmodern, may they come in numbers. "Artists and writers must be brought back into the bosom of the community, or at least, if the latter is considered to be ill, they must be assigned the task of healing it" (p. 73).

Throughout his body of work, Campbell consistently reminds his readers that any "seeing" of the ineffable, any apprehension of the Absolute, must first come in the form of local stories from our own, often ill, communities. Such stories about *living* journeys are our only means of connection to the universal. Put another way, self-actualization comes only when we are able to enter into society with unique renderings of our lived experience. Similarly, Walter Fisher (1985) contends that human beings are inherently *homonarrans*. We construct self, other and the world in which we "exist" through narrative processes. Fisher has been criticized, however, for implicitly suggesting a meta-narrative in his conception of *homonarrans*. Perhaps via Lyotard's position we might re-name ourselves *heteronarrans*, implying that one story cannot and should not serve as the totality of experience (as if totality could be achieved) for all persons. Local narratives are particularly important for marginalized voices that cannot tell their stories in accord with the grand narratives produced by dominant groups. To be able to articulate one's own experience on one's own terms is vital not only for fostering the diversity of perspectives operating within a given culture, but it is also necessary for praxis-oriented communications within an ethic of care.

Supporting this vision, Campbell (1988) suggests that "What we are looking for in these creation [or narrative] stories is a way of experiencing the world that will open to us the transcendent that informs it, and at the same time forms ourselves within it. That is what people want. That is what the soul asks for" (p. 52). And Thomas Moore (1992) reminds us, in order to care for the soul, we must nurture its expressions:

> We know soul is being cared for when our pleasures feel deeper than usual, when we can let go of the need to be free of complexity and confusion, and when compassion takes the place of distrust and fear. Soul is interested in the differences among cultures and individuals, and with ourselves it wants to be expressed in uniqueness if not in outright eccentricity. (pp. 304-5)

Through such nourishment, we live in the Spirit with other beings. This spiritual affection is revealed through *narrative communication* with an *other*. According to Burke (1969), this spiritual affection was the expression of love that Socrates was trying to advocate in his dialogues: "And it is the living, *spoken* word that would be the completest form of love, as thus transformed into the corresponding interlockings of verbal interchange" (p. 425). For only through conversation with another, then, do we truly enact our *purpose*. Our individual voices, our rhetorics, come together through narrative to yield a "heightened consciousness," the possibility for transformation, transcendence, and rebirth, or the following of Campbell's hero-path. "*I* and *Thou* take their stand not merely in relation, but also in the solid give-and-take of talk," says Buber. "Here alone [these moment of relations], then, as reality that cannot be lost, are gazing and being gazed upon, knowing and being known, loving and being loved" (p. 103). With this, the multiplicity of our heteroglossic narratives (see Bakhtin, 1981) through the solid give-and-take of talk leads us to a final plateau of this rhizome.

Toward a Communicative Ethics through Multi-Disciplinary Scholarship

Often people live within local mythologies with no sense of self. Mary Nicolini (1994), in her article, "Stories Can Save Us: A Defense of Narrative Writing," illuminates the power of the personal narrative. She addresses the problem of bright yet bored students losing interest in academic pursuits they may not be able to relate to. Nicolini asks: "The best lessons build on students' strengths, but when are students asked to write about that which they are experts on: themselves?" (p. 56). But how can we build on students' strengths without opening the doors to multi-disciplinary scholarship? Part and parcel of the creative struggle (within academia) involves examining the best ways, the most effective ways, to expose students to their own multiplicitous selves and the multiplicitous selves of *others* with whom they share their *spaces* and *stories* in our society. Interdisciplinarity and cross-cultural studies, then, are two concepts central to establishing a communicative ethics and are key in establishing how teachers across disciplines can discover the most helpful and most effective ways that students can learn about themselves, others, and the world. Marjorie Pryse (1998), arguing for the inclusion of various feminist discourses in a multi-disciplinary curriculum suggests that:

> Feminist scholars and teachers can contribute to such a future – in which the *mestiza* intellectual works, in Adrienne Rich's 1975 vision, "toward a woman-centered university," by consciously including/ "incorporating" in our own thinking and teaching the work of feminist scholars that has emerged from other disciplines. . . . It means including narrative and poetry as integral to feminist theory. . . asking non-Spanish-speaking students to struggle with the language borders Anzaldua, Lugones, and Maria Luisa "Papusa" Molina cross in their work. . . . helping students who have avoided science since high school to understand what Sandra Harding means when she explains "Why 'Physics' is a Bad Model for Physics". . . choosing textbooks and anthologies that highlight interdisciplinarity; and in particular challenging students to read writers whose work crosses cultural as well as disciplinary difference, such as Patricia Williams and Peggy Sanday. (p.17)

An interdisciplinary, cross-cultural approach to communication, philosophy and qualitative studies writ large reminds us as teachers and scholars that ". . .*it is one's culture and one's society that one is looking at*" (see Lugones, 1993, p. 50, original emphasis). Therefore, we cannot undertake either research or pedagogy from an impartial stance. If we do, we run the risk of reproducing metanarratives about communicative ethics that already characterize a large portion of mainstream scholarly discourse and perpetuate the exclusion of marginalized others. Interdisciplinary and multicultural ways of thinking about the world through narrative have helped me to become a more effective instructor as well as a more wholistic researcher. They continue to remind me that I am speaking for and to a living audience.

Schrag (1986), more so than Deleuze or Foucault, retrieves the subject, the *self*, as a viable and integral part of the communicative praxis necessary for multi-disciplinary pedagogy. He states, "This hermeneutical self-implicature of the subject proceeds in tandem with the rhetorical turn, in which discourse and action are disclosed not only as being *by* someone but also *for* and *to* someone" (p. 214). Surely the "other" in any communicative situation must also be recognized as an agent (a *self*) capable of introducing both intentional and unintentional discourse, action, or a shift of power relations into that given situation. Schrag (1997) points out a problematic tendency in both Deleuze's politics of desire and Foucault's ontology of power. "This is the tendency to valorize and celebrate the dynamics of desire and the effects of power at the expense of the role of rationality in the life of the self-constituting subject" (p. 56). He offers a corrective by recognizing the phenomenological notion of "functioning intentionality" as "the concretely functioning intentionality that is operative in embodied communicative practices" (p. 57). We must remember that our students each have "functioning intentionalities" of their own: they are not merely empty receptacles wherein we, as teachers, deposit information. This intentionality describes our bodily comprehension of the world as much as our mental or psychological comprehension. In all communicative interactions, we enter as selves with a "dynamics of discernment, an economy of practical wisdom that exhibits its own insight without needing to wait on the determinations of pure cognition and pure theory"(p. 57). It is this type of "practical wisdom" that orients us to the pragmatics of daily affairs and being in the world with others. Wouldn't we be remiss to neglect this reality of our existence, especially when we are in the role of *teacher*?

Schrag, able to tranform the "unity" at issue for Deleuze, which "is always within this dimension of transversality, in which unity and totality are established for themselves, without unifying or totalizing objects or subjects," suggests an ethical vision for the self after postmodernity (p. 57). The unity *is* a unity of difference and plurality, and yet this combined difference and plurality does not reduce the self to a nothingness or suggest that it might be "discovered in totality." Schrag's tranversality is a welcomed view of the self in discourse, action, community and transcendence, much like Bakhtin's notion of the transgredience that makes up our individual selves and Buber's description of the self as whole only when she is speaking her *Thou*. Moreover, Schrag's notion of transcendence speaks to pedagogical concerns about the need for a multi-disciplinary way of being-in-the-classroom:

> Transcendence in its threefold function as a principle of protest against cultural hegemony, as a condition for a transversal unification

that effects a convergence without coincidence, and as a power of giving without expectation of return [an ethic of care extended beyond self to others], stands outside the economies of science, morality, art, and religion as culture-spheres. This defines transcendence as a robust alterity. (1997, p. 148)

Schrag's notion of transcendence can be adopted as an eloquent and contemporary (though quite historical indeed) way of envisioning a communicative ethics across the fields of philosophy, communication and the social sciences. By seeing the capacity for multi-disciplinary scholarship to provide "robust alterities" for the study of the human condition, scholars can articulate that which is vital to postmodern, pragmatic, feminist and, most importantly, humane understandings of the disparate ways of knowing and being in the world.

The purposes of such a curriculum would not be to "discover" which "field" is on the top of the institutional hierarchy, but rather to address the *abstract machine* that sweeps us along the academic plateau. There are many rhizomes layered over and over each other that need to be uncovered – rhizomes of administration, of learning, of finance, of politics, of the media, of sports and entertainment, of personal relationships, and of resistance movements which connect and spread like crabgrass. We need to follow them to saturation. They send out "transformational multiplicities" that are too rarely seen, named, or understood. By and large, academia continues to operate under the dictums of the State market apparatus where minoritarian words are not received favorably. Yet, Deleuze and Guattari would encourage such discursive strategies, especially in academia. This vision can be actualized through a multi-disciplinary curriculum.

Clearly, the thinkers whose discourses have informed this narrative on the basis for a communicative ethics represent a variety of disciplines and their concomitant perspectives. Philosophers, Literary Theorists, Dialogicians, Rhetorical Scholars, and one eager student can speak together in a multi-disciplinary text such as this. They may find "convergence without coincidence" herein. It is only through my own multi-disciplinary education both in and out of the academy, an education that I experience as a blessing and am therefore humbled by, that I was able by way of this narrative to advance an argument for a communicative ethics that extends while acknowledging my own religious orientation. I have tried to locate "convergences" and connect them to the Whole, to an energy source larger than any single voice could hope to be. Faith in God, in the world, and in others has brought me to where and who and how I am. But the journey continues, and the rhizome is once again moving toward a rupture.

Despite all of the potential restrictions upon the *self*, the self after postmodernity continues to make choices. What I have sought to contribute to a discussion of how this self should proceed ethically, is to relate what I believe in, what I value. I value saying what you mean and standing in those words. I believe in living within an ethic of care that allows others the same concerns and opportunities. I realize, as Joseph Campbell did, that "the privilege of a lifetime is being who you are." That said, I will temporary leap from this plateau for cultivating a communicative ethics only for it to be re-opened on some other plateau, by some other question about the human condition. I would like to leave my readers with a portion of a poem from Campbell as it appears in Diane Osbon's (1991) *Reflections on the Art of Living: A Joseph Campbell Companion*. For me, the expressive and soothing words of this poem exemplify an ethical *self* in discourse, action, community and transcendence. It is a poem that I always try to fly out with:

> *Our own life lives on the acts of other people.* [Emphasis mine]
> If you are lifeworthy, you can take it.
> Follow your bliss.
> The heroic life is living the *individual* adventure.
> There is no security in following the call to adventure
> [the call to consciousness, the call to the *other*]
> Nothing is exciting if you know what the outcome is going to be.
> To refuse the call means stagnation.
> What you don't experience positively you will experience negatively.
> You enter the forest at the darkest point, where there is no path.
> Where there is a way or path, it is someone else's path.
> If you follow someone else's way,
> you are not going to realize your potential.
> The goal of the hero trip down to the jewel point
> is to find those levels in the psyche
> that open, open, open,
> and finally open to the mystery of your Self being
> Buddha consciousness
> or the Christ.
> That's the journey.
> It is all about finding that still point in our mind
> where commitment drops away.
> I believe it is through living with others that we experience and communicate
> the spirit and dwell ethically together in the world . . . Amen.

References

Bakhtin, M. M. (1981). *The dialogic imagination.* (C. Emerson & M. Holquist, Trans.) Austin: University of Texas Press.

Bakhtin, M. M. (1993). *Toward a philosophy of the act.* (V. Liapunov, Trans.) M. Holoquist, Ed. Austin: University of Texas Press.

Buber, M. (1958). *I and Thou.* New York: Charles Scribner's Sons, 2nd ed.

Burke, K. (1984). *Permanence and change.* Berkeley: University of California Press, 3rd ed.

Burke, K. (1970). *The rhetoric of religion: Studies in logology.* Berkeley: University of California Press.

Burke, K. (1966). *Language as symbolic action: Essays on life, literature and method.* Berkeley: University of California Press.

Campbell, J. (1973). *Myths to live by.* New York: Bantam.

Campbell, J., with Bill Moyers. (1988). *The power of myth.* New York: Doubleday.

Carr, D. (1986). *Time, narrative, and history.* Bloomington: Indiana University Press.

Code, Lorraine. (1993). Taking subjectivity into account. In L. Alcoff and Elizabeth Potter (Eds), *Feminist Epistemologies (pp. 15-43).* New York: Routledge.

Deleuze, G. & Guattari, F. (1987). *A Thousand Plateaus: Capitalism and schizophrenia.* Minneapolis: Minnesota University Press.

Fisher, W. R. (1985). The narrative paradigm: In the Beginning. *Journal of Communication, 35,* 174-89.

Foucault, M. (1995). *Discipline and punish: Birth of the prison.* (A. Sheridan, Trans.). New York: Random House.

Heidegger, M. (1993). *Basic writings.* D. F. Krell, ed. San Francisco: HarperCollins.

Holoquist, M. (1990). *Dialogism : Bakhtin and his world.* New York: Routledge.

Husserl, E. (1931). The Thesis of the Natural Standpoint and Its Suspension, and "On Eidectic Reduction," as both texts appear in the course packet of readings for my class *Deconstruction and Postmodern Thought,* taken Fall 1999, directed by Calvin O. Schrag.

Lyotard, J. F. (1991). *The postmodern condition.* (Geoff Bennington and Brian Massumi, Trans.). Minneapolis: University of Minnesota Press.

Moore, T. (1992). *Care of the soul.* New York: HarperCollins.

Nicolini, M. B. (1994). Stories can save us: A defense of narrative writing. *English Journal, 83,* 56-61.

Osbon, Diane. (1991). *Reflections on the art of living: A Joseph Campbell companion.* New York: HarperCollins.

Pryse, M. (1998). *Critical Interdisciplinarity, Women's Studies, and Cross-Cultural Insight. NWSA Journal,* Spring.

Schrag, C. O. (1997*). The self after postmodernity.* New Haven: Yale University Press.

Schrag, C. O. (1986). *Communicative praxis and the space of subjectivity.* Bloomington: Indiana University Press.

Chapter 7

Discerning How We'll Move Together Through Spiritual And Communicative Practice

Kathleen D. Clark
University of Akron

Abstract

This essay argues that communicative practices that are attentive and responsive to dimension(s) of reality referenced by the terms spirituality or spiritual may provide a solution to the inadequate use of organizational mission statements. I argue that social structuring of collectivities of individual humans, such as the form we recognize as being an organization, is a human invention that suppresses and privileges attention paid to various aspects of reality, as all human inventions do, with various intended and unintended consequences. Reintegrating such dimension(s) of reality referenced by spirituality can expand the utility of communicative practices for organizations, particularly in the area of managing organizational mission. My presumption is that organizational processes can be made more humane, responsive, and ultimately more productive. A Christian contemplative discernment process for social systems provides an exemplar of how attention to more dimensions of reality may provide a more realistic, and thus more useful, basis for determining and articulating organizational mission statements.

In this essay, I would like to argue that understanding the dimension(s) of reality referenced by the construct *spirituality* can expand the utility of communicative practices for organizations, particularly in the area of managing organizational mission. My exploration is based on the presumption that organizational processes can be made more humane, responsive, and ultimately more productive by attending to such dimensions of reality.

To begin this discussion, I review critiques in the management theory and organizational management communication literature on the use of mission statements by organizations. Next, I posit reasons for the inadequacy of organizational mission statements, proceeding to suggest that communicative practices which are attentive and responsive to dimension(s) of reality referenced by *spirituality* have the potential to create vibrant and useful articulations of organizational mission. Additionally, I am informed by my familiarity with contemplative spiritual practices [1], so I conclude this essay with an exemplar of the communicative practices of one organizational discernment process that is attentive and responsive to dimension(s) of reality referenced by *spirituality*.

The following two sections provide context for evaluating the exemplar. Noted management theorists grapple with the gap between ideal and actual organizational mission statements. Next, I explicate the constructs that underpin my argument, such as the notion of dimension(s) of reality referenced by spirituality, a communication-as-procedure approach to communicative practice, the notion of socially structuring through communicative practice, and the potential for organizational adaptation implied by human inventiveness in response to changing situations.

Management Theorists

Research by organizational communication researchers Gail Fairhurst, and colleagues, and Alan Belasen documents the discrepancies between an organization's mission statement, and the reality of its everyday workings. They note that organizations vary widely in their conception of what a mission statement is, and even in having a clear sense of mission at all. Added to that confusion is the complexity of what is actually communicated to employees and how the employees understand their role in the organization. The picture that emerges is of a collectivity of individuals muddling along together, possibly in the same direction, and possibly in the intended direction.

Management theorist Andrew Campbell (1992) argues that for many organizations the idea and practice of mission is shallow, poorly understood and erratically followed. He describes two characteristic schools of thought about the role of mission in business organizations,

The strategy school views mission primarily as a strategic tool, an intellectual discipline that defines the business's commercial rationale and target market. Mission is something that is linked to strategy but at a higher level. In this context, it is perceived as the first step in strategic management. It exists to answer two fundamental questions: 'What is our business and what should it be? . . . . In contrast, the second school of thought argues that mission is the cultural 'glue' that enables an organization to function as a collective unity. This cultural glue consists of strong norms and values that influence the ways that people behave, how they work together, and how they pursue the goals of the organization. This form of mission can amount to a business philosophy that helps employees to perceive and interpret events in the same way and to speak a common language. Compared with the strategic view of mission, this interpretation sees mission as capturing some of the emotional aspects of the organization. It is concerned with generating cooperation among employees through shared values and standards of behavior. (Campbell, 1992, pp.12-13)

Campbell concludes thusly based on his experience and research into management development:

> One question that always comes up is where the company is going and what it stands for…. With the amount of practice that chief executives get, you would think that they would be very good at answering this question. But they are not. Their answers rarely get close to the concern that gave rise to the question; managers are frequently left unsatisfied. What managers are searching for is a sense of purpose and a sense of identity, something that we are going to call…a 'sense of mission.' They want more from their organizations than pay, security, and the opportunity to develop their skills. They want a cause that is personally satisfying. (Campbell, 1992, p. 1)

Thus, we see a gap between the way that organizations operate and the way they would like to operate, and confusion about how to improve this state of affairs.

In the groundbreaking book, *The Fifth Discipline*, Peter Senge and colleagues suggest a solution. They draw upon systems theory to articulate their conception of building a learning organization, one that incorporates personal mastery in order to create desired results. Such mastery includes, reflection upon one's and the organization's mental models to understand how these shape actions and decisions, collective building of a sense of shared vision, transformation of conversational and thinking skills through team learning, and learning systems thinking in order to understand the forces and interrelationships of natural and economic systems.

However, Flood (2000) critiques Senge et al.'s widely touted approach. He argues that the use of systemic theory by Senge and colleagues is inherently flawed because although the theory is descriptive of reality, it does not suggest how to change organizational procedures in such a way that the organization, the system, is changed in a desired direction. Flood (2000) writes:

> System dynamics does model emergent phenomenon, but it does not model the emergent process. It does present interdisciplinary principles, but it does not extend them to principles of cybernetic viability. It does suggest the need for a participatory structure but it does not offer one. It does offer principles for action, but it does not deliver principles for action research...what is needed is an appreciation of systemic thinking that meaningfully addresses both the concerns *of* system dynamics and the concerns *with* system dynamics. (p. 73)

Thus, we see a call for more clarity and intentionality about how organizations function as well as the remaining challenge to make mission and mission statements viable to significantly guide their organization. The range of perspectives articulated above suggest that such theorists are continuing to try to deal with the complex, dynamic, vast nature of the reality within which groupings of individuals trying to move collectively toward some objective. They establish the extent to which relevant reality is often inadequately addressed by organizations both in terms of understanding mission and the individuals whose routine behaviors constitute the organization.

I want to argue that organizational theorists would be helped if they took a few steps *back* and considered what must be considered *before* one begins to deal with managing an organization's mission. In the following section, I will move through various constructs in order to suggest a different way to think about what is happening in organizations. It does not negate the insights of systems theory, but it may address some of the problems discussed about how to work with the reality of an organization in such a way that meaningful and sustainable change may take place.

Constructs

The argument of this essay rests on four constructs about human behavior and capability: we structure socially through patterned communicative practice, we structure in response to the situations in which we find ourselves, we are capable of inventing and reinventing social structuring, and *spirituality* references dimension(s) of reality often ignored and/or suppressed by social structuring. Thus, humans are capable of inventing patterned communicative practices for the use of organizational mission statements that will create more attentive and responsive social structuring to such dimension(s) of reality.

Communicative practice

A fundamental premise of this essay is that social structuring is accomplished through patterned communicative practices (Clark, 1999; Dervin & Clark, 1993; Dervin, 1993). It would actually be more accurate to call these practices *communicative procedurings* because the fundamental idea is that communication is a process made up of many acts of communicating, both internal and external.

A communication-as-procedure perspective focuses on the hows of structuring through communicatings. Following Carter (1991, 1989, 1980), communicatings may include internal acts (e.g., modes of observing, categorizing, defining, labeling, summarizing) and external acts (e.g., modes of writing, hearing, talking, joining, gesturing). Each of these communicatings can be seen as a step or series of steps, formal or informal, habitualized or newly invented. Some of these steps repeat the past while others break with the past. These behaviors apply to relating to self (e.g., remembering, forgetting, making up one's mind, changing one's mind), and to others (e.g., loving, hating, deciding, disagreeing). They apply to relating to individuals when seen independently as well as when constrained or limited by or enjoined by a collectivity. All of these behaviors are driven by the only site that directly drives behavior—individual human agency (which may be operating consciously or unconsciously).

In looking at communication in this way, it is important to conceptualize the procedurings as occurring in time-space as a series of step-takings which can be internal or external, overt or subtle. In observing any situation, some of these procedurings are recurrent and routinized, others are not. The repeated use of routinized communicatings is conceptualized as stabilizing both messages and structural forms long enough in time-space for identifiable patterns to be observable. But if all communicatings were routinized there could be no change or resistance or struggle.

Part of the impetus of taking on a communication-as-procedure perspective is to incorporate time and space into research design and thus be able to look at both stability over time and change over time. Depending on the particular confluence of interests of the researcher, stability might be alternately conceptualized as repetition, rigidity, and habit while change might be alternately conceptualized as flexibility, innovation, or caprice. Since few human actions are innate, these communication procedures are conceptualized as invented at moments in time-space, often repeated, sometimes borrowed, and sometimes reinvented, challenged, or even transcended by other procedurings. Thus, a communication-as-procedure analytic makes it possible to observe both inventing and reinventing responses to situations because it directs attention to procedurings, seeing them as energizings used to shape the situation of an individual or a collectivity.

Social structuring

The use of a communication-as-procedure perspective is grounded in one of the meta-theoretic foundations of Sense-Making Methodology. As a perspective, it is informed in particular by Giddens' structuration theory and the theoretical work of Richard Carter. Giddens (1984) argues that it is routinized, reiterated human activities through which societal structures are enacted. Carter (1991, 1989, 1980), however, contends that collective behavior proceeds by and in step taking, and calls for inventive approaches to the study and design of step-taking behavior in seeking the well-being of humanity. For the purposes of this research, the term social structuring is used to imply that humans invent and maintain social structure, and are in a position to stop giving energy to one structuring, and to begin giving it to another.

Invention and reinvention

Dervin and Clark (1993, 1989) and Dervin (1999, 1993) contend that since social structuring is apparent in communicative procedures, any intentional change must attend to such procedures, both to discontinue no longer desired ones and to begin anew. Theorizing grounded in a communication-as-procedure perspective posits that attention to the invention and reinvention of communicative procedures opens a window onto the dynamic behaviors that create, maintain, reinvent, and discontinue social structurings. Of particular concern is the difficulty and promise of bringing to awareness communicative procedures that have become habitual and thus invisible. Dervin and Clark (1989) argue that ignorance of habitual communicative procedures is likely to sabotage efforts to change social structurings. Further, bringing habitual communicative procedures to awareness is defined as a necessary step in reinventing more situationally responsive structurings. Dervin and Clark emphasize, following Carter, that this potential for invention and reinvention is assumed to be inherently characteristic of human beings. In short, what humans structure they can potentially change but attention to communication-as-procedure is necessary to do so (although certainly not sufficient).

Dimension(s) of reality referenced by spirituality

Based on a definition of spirituality inductively derived from an ethnographic study of small group process in a women's spirituality group (Clark, 1999), and further clarified and informed by the assumptions about reality underlying spiritual direction (Dougherty, 1995; Farnham et al., 1994; Liebert, 1996; Mostyn, 1996;), I posit that people often use the term *spirituality* to refer to levels or dimensions of reality not usually included in social structuring. I specifically want to cultivate the notion that a defining characteristic of this spiritual reality is that it underlies and upholds social structuring, rather like an aquifer lies under the ground humans inhabit, providing a necessary resource for all human activities. I want to challenge the notion that the spiritual can be compartmentalized as one possible, intangible and often neglected realm of human activity.

Some collectivities of individuals have already socially structured themselves into organizations that attend to dimension(s) of reality referenced by *spirituality*. For hundreds of years, members of some Christian orders have used contemplative spiritual practices to discern mission for themselves (Dougherty, 1995; Farnham et al., 1994; Mostyn, 1996) by paying explicit attention to these dimension(s) of reality. In the discussion of the exemplar below, it becomes clear that it is routine in contemplative collective discernment to use communicative practices in order to create a space, a social structuring that is attentive and responsive to dimension(s) of reality referenced by *spirituality*.

Conclusion

Structuring collectivities of individuals in the social form we recognize as an organization is the result of human invention in response to a situation. Further, such social structuring is accomplished through communicative practices. With their iterative patterns, communicative practices suppress and privilege attention paid to, and value placed on, aspects of reality with various intended and unintended consequences for the collectivity of individuals being structured into an organization. I believe that the dimension(s) of reality referenced by the terms *spiritual* or *spirituality* are some that are routinely silenced by the communicative practices that structure most organizations, religious or secular, particularly in North America.

One implication that follows from this argument is that intentionally attending to the dimension(s) of collectively experienced reality referenced by *spirituality* may provide a meaningful and pragmatically useful focus for managing organizations. At the least, such a focus would make management more reality based, even if it chose not to address this area of reality. However, the potential for management by attending and responding to more of reality for the individuals who comprise it would seem to have far-reaching and beneficial consequences.

A second implication is that if a certain social structuring is something invented by humans, then it is something that can be adapted, abandoned, or reinvented by humans. Therefore, humans are capable of reinventing social structuring to incorporate attention and responsiveness to the dimension(s) of collectively experienced reality referenced by *spirituality*. In terms of organizations, then, we may conclude that *not* attending to all of the reality being experienced by the collectivity of individuals comprising the organization will hamper a useful and realistic determination of organizational mission.

Notes

[1] The author is currently working toward the Diploma in the Art of Spiritual Direction from the San Francisco Theological Seminary (Presbyerian Church (USA)). The particular mode of contemplative spirituality used in this essay is based on that program's interpretation.

References

Belasen, A. T. (2000). *Leading the learning organization: Communication and competencies for managing change.* Albany, NY: State University of New York Press.

Campbell, A., Nash, L.L. (1992). *A sense of mission: Defining direction for the large organization.* New York: Addison-Wesley Publishing Company.

Carter, R. F. (1991). Comparative analysis, theory, and cross-cultural communication. *Communication Theory, 1,* 151-159.

Carter, R. F. (1989, May). What does a gap imply? Paper prepared for panel, *Finding a more powerful analytic for comparative research: Using the gap idea in cross-cultural research,* Intercultural and Development Communication Division, International Communication Association meeting, San Francisco, CA.

Carter, R. F. (1980, December). *Discontinuity and communication.* Paper written for the seminar on communication from Eastern and Western sponsored by the East-West Communication Institute, East-West Center, Honolulu, HI.

Clark, K.D. (1999, December). A communication-as-procedure perspective on a women's spirituality group: A Sense-Making and ethnographic exploration of communicative proceduring in feminist small group process. *The Electronic Journal of Communication / La Revue Electronique de Communication, 9* (2, 3, 4). [On-line] Available: http://www.cios.org/www/ejc/v9n23499.htm

Dervin, B. (1999, in press). On studying information needs and seeking methodologically: The implications of connecting meta-theory and method. *Information Processing and Management.*

Dervin, B. (1993). Verbing communication: Mandate for disciplinary invention. *Journal of Communication, 43,* 45-54.

Dervin, B., Clark, K. D. (1993). Communication and democracy: Mandate for procedural invention. In S. Splichal & J. Wasko (Eds.) *Communication and democracy.* Norwood, NJ: Ablex.

Dervin, B., & Clark, K. D. (1989). Communication as cultural identity: the invention mandate. *Media Development 2,* 5-8.

Dougherty, R. M. (1995). *Group spiritual direction: Community for discernment.* New York/Mahwah, NJ: Paulist Press.

Fairhurst, G. T., Jordan, J. M., & Neuwirth, K. (1997). Why are we here? Managing the meaning of an organizational mission statement. *Journal of Applied Communication Research, 25,* 243-263.

Farnham, S. G., Gill, J. P., McLean, R. T., & Ward, S. M. (1994).

Listening hearts: Discerning call in community (Revised edition). Harrisburg, PA: Morehouse Publishing.

Flood, R. L. (1999). *Rethinking the Fifth Discipline: Learning within the unknowable.* London/New York: Routledge.

Giddens, A. (1984). Structuration theory, empirical research and social critique. In The constitution of society (pp.281-354). Berkeley/Los Angeles, CA: University of California Press.

Liebert, E. (1996, January). *Art of discernment.* Lectures presented at the Certificate in the Art of Spiritual Direction, San Francisco Theological Seminary, San Anselmo, CA.

McKinley, A., Starkey, K. (1998). *Foucault, management and organization theory: From panopticon to technologies of self.* London/Thousand Oaks, CA: Sage.

Mostyn, J. (1996, January). *Integrating spirituality and social structures.* Lectures presented at the Certificate in the Art of Spiritual Direction, San Francisco Theological Seminary, San Anselmo, CA.

Senge, P., Kleiner, A., Roberts, C., Ross, R., Roth, G. & Smith, B. (1999). *The dance of change: The challenges to sustaining momentum in learning organizations: A Fifth Discipline resource.* New York: Currency/Doubleday.

Senge, P., Roberts, C., Ross, R., Roth, G. & Smith, B. Kleiner, A., (1994). *The Fifth Discipline fieldbook: Strategies and tools for building a learning organization.* New York: Currency/Doubleday.

Chapter 8

Social Capital, Spirituality and the Value of Communication

Andrew P. Herman
Northwestern University

Abstract

This chapter examines the relationship between spirituality, social capital, and communication. After introducing Coleman's (1988) concept of social capital as a set of "obligations and expectations, information channels, and social norms" that allow citizens to fulfill their needs and desires in society, I discuss the application of this notion to religious organizations. I argue that the unique spiritual nature of these organizations is often ignored, limiting the application of the theory. Spirituality is important to social capital because it imposes on social actors concepts of motivation, encouragement, and accountability. Potential areas of new research are proposed for communication scholars to further understand the special relationship between spirituality and social capital.

Coleman's (1988) notion of social capital has been applied to a variety of situations across numerous contexts (e.g., Coleman, 1988; Foley & Edwards, 1997, 1998; Greeley, 1997; McRoberts, 1999; Wood, 1994, 1997). While arguments have been developed that indicate the positive effect religion has on social capital (Coleman, 1988; Greeley, 1997, 1999; Ladd, 1998; McRoberts, 1999; Roof, 1996; Wood, 1994, 1997), there has been limited theorizing that religion, as a spiritual activity, could be a unique variable within the framework of social capital.

This limited perspective on the significant and unique role of spirituality has left a void in our conceptual framework of social capital. What is apparent is that most discussions of social capital underestimate the potential influence that spirituality has in the life and work of any active religious organization. The significance that spirituality might play in the actors' lives is often ignored, leaving room for communication research to show more clearly how a community's spirituality influences its use of social capital. As to why many scholars miss or downplay the relation between social capital and spirituality, Wade Clark Roof (1996) makes an astute observation:

Our discipline has been impoverished by an uncritical acceptance of an epistemological tradition in which things of the spirit have been radically split from material things, and in which mind is treated as utterly separate from body... Implicit in this approach is the tendency to objectify religion; in so doing, sociology of religion forfeits the possibility of grasping the dynamic, experiential, subjectively meaningful, emotionally exciting, indeterminate, motivating, and active aspects of religion. (p. 161)

Seemingly, the strong secular nature that undergirds the Western worldview has limited our ability to see beyond the literal structures of our religious organizations to the spiritual structures; to see the forces and motivations that may be at work in the members. As Wood (1997) notes, "contemporary political sociology typically treats religion as a residual category, unimportant except insofar as it provides material resources or social legitimacy for a movement" (p. 397). No doubt, this blindspot has cut short our ability to notice the dynamics of social capital in religious groups. On the other hand, however, examples can be found where researchers are attempting to make sense of the spiritual aspects of organizations and their influence on the organizations' display of social capital. Wood (1994, 1997) provides interesting examples of spirituality and religion moving beyond the simple social structures of the organization, to recognizing that there is the possibility of a source of power and accountability beyond the organization itself.

Social Capital

Coleman (1988) sought to reconcile two divergent intellectual understandings for what constitutes social action. One, more sociological in nature, understood actors to be social beings, shaped and directed by the surrounding norms and obligations. The other approach was from an economic perspective that considered the actor an independent, rational entity striving to fulfill his or her own self-interests. Coleman argued that both of these approaches had some strengths, but also some limitations. To accommodate these differences, Coleman (1988), conceived of *social capital,* a notion that attempts to place a rational actor within the confines of a social structural understanding of society. Coleman desired to balance the strongly individualistic tendencies of the rational actor with the reality that the rational actor lives within the context of social structures and influences. Thus, Coleman recognized that we as individuals can make decisions that either comply with or go against the prevailing social mores of the time. Out of this balancing act was born the notion of social capital, the "obligations and expectations, information channels, and social norms" that allow citizens to fulfill their needs and desires in society (Coleman, 1988, p. S95).

An important aspect of social capital is that it exists for the purpose of communal facilitation:

> Social capital is defined by its function. It is not a single entity but a variety of different entities, with two elements in common: they all consist of some aspect of social structures, and they facilitate certain actions of actors—whether persons or corporate actors—within the structure. (p. S98)

It is this functional approach to community that makes the present discussion important. As Coleman points out, social capital does not consist of a single entity. Rather, any number of influences might come to bear on the organizational structure and its members. More importantly, these entities are facilitating (or perhaps constraining), in some way, the actions of the members of the organization. For example, Coleman (1988) marvels at the wholesale diamond market that exists in New York City, where merchants regularly exchange large amounts of diamonds for inspection solely on the basis of interpersonal trust. They have no insurance on the diamonds and no guarantees that another merchant would not swap diamonds for his advantage. Coleman (1988) concludes that "close ties, through family, community, and religious affiliation, provide

the insurance that is necessary to facilitate the transactions in the market"
(p. 99). These are the entities that facilitate the merchants to interact
honestly with one another.

However, I question whether these close ties, as interconnected as
they may be in the relatively closed, Jewish diamond merchant
community, are the only entities that are facilitating the actions of these
merchants. Certainly, the merchants' religious affiliation—the fact that
they all attend the same synagogue—can have a powerful influence on
their behavior. But what if they all attended the same country club or
sports facility? Would those relationships promote the same level of trust
as the synagogue membership?

Communication's Role

Trenholm and Jensen (2000) define communication as "the process
whereby humans collectively create and regulate social reality" (p. 5). In
discussing their definition, Trenholm and Jensen emphasize some points
that are pertinent for addressing spirituality and social capital. One is that
when we communicate, we create a social reality concerning both physical
and non-physical objects. Our communication typically does not cause an
object to come into being (unless we were involved in its actual creation),
but it still influences how we view and understand that object in our social
context. This is true of symbolic concepts as well, which comprise a
significant amount of a person's spiritual understanding. Ultimately, how
we talk about these physical and symbolic realities influences their
integration into our personal lives and the broader religious community.
Simultaneously, we also regulate our social reality through communication
(Trenholm & Jensen, 2000). The creative and regulatory force of
communication becomes especially important when considering the role of
spirituality in social capital. How community members talk about their
religious faith and how they approach the various social issues before them
influences their perception of reality. At this point, communication
becomes the connective tissue between spirituality and social capital. As
Trenholm and Jensen (2000) point out, communication is a human process
that is done in the collective, which is an underlying component of social
capital (Bourdieu, 1986; Coleman, 1988). As people interact with one
another, a corporate understanding is created that influences all the
participants' perceptions and responses. Through communication, a
spiritual component is infused into the faith community's social capital;
one that should exhibit patterns of supernatural motivation and

accountability. It is this infusion of spirituality that makes the faith community unique in its utilization of social capital.

Conclusion

Coleman never intended to focus specifically on the role of religion in his original examples of social capital, subsequent studies have been more deliberate in their use of religious structures as an example of significant social capital. However, as a whole, many of these studies do not appreciate or consider the special contribution a spiritual worldview can provide to an organization's social capital. It is unclear if this is a weakness of Coleman's (1988) model, or an inevitability of the general naturalistic worldview that predominates Western scholarship. Either way, within a spiritual framework, issues of organizational authority, accountability, and motivation become important variables that need to be considered. That is, when the concept of God becomes part of the organization's view of the world, its perception of any situation should become significantly different from that of an organization without this spiritual component. Fortunately, studies are appearing that have begun to explore this important variable (McRoberts, 1999; Wood, 1994, 1997).

One exciting prospect of this growing recognition of the importance of studying the role of spirituality in organizational theory is how communication scholarship can contribute to current research. A spiritual perspective introduces the idea that an organization should be working within the framework of a higher authority placing specific expectations on the group, all the while encouraging them toward a goal. A basic understanding of the role of communication in supplying a connection between spirituality and social capital has already been discussed. However, communication theory raises further questions as to how individual religious communities operate within this framework. For example, Are there different ways in which spirituality is communicated? Can different communication styles be observed within or between any groups based on gender, age, culture or theology? Just how does each religious community communicate these important aspects of God to its members? Another topic to consider would be the correlation between communication, spirituality, social capital, and fulfilled goals. After communication patterns within these organizations are identified, there needs to be an analysis to consider if this "spiritual communication" is truly having a positive effect. These are just a few examples of how communication scholarship could help inform the role of religion and spirituality in the study of social capital. Hopefully, through the process of considering these questions, we will more fully appreciate the continued significance of Coleman's (1988) concept of social capital as well as the role spirituality plays in it.

References

Bourdieu, P. (1986). The forms of social capital. In J. Richardson (Ed.), *Handbook of theory and research for the sociology of education* (pp. 241-258). New York: Greenwood Press.

Coleman, J. (1988). Social capital in the creation of human capital. *American Journal of Sociology, 94,* S95-S120.

Foley M., & Edwards, B.. (1997). Social capital, civil society and contemporary democracy. *American Behavioral Scientist, 40.*

Foley M., & Edwards, B. (Eds.). (1998). *Beyond Tocqueville: Civil society and social capital in comparative perspective.* American Behavioral Scientist, 42(1).

Greeley, A. (1999). *The other civic America, religion and social capital.* The American Prospect, 32, May-June 1997. [Online]. Available: http://www.prospect.org/cgi-bin/printable.cgi. [2000, February 28].

Greeley, A. (1997). *Coleman revisited: Religious structures as a source of social capital.* American Behavioral Scientist, 40(5), 587-594.

McRoberts, O. (1999). *Understanding the "new" black Pentecostal activism: Lessons from ecumenical urban ministries in Boston.* Sociology of Religion, 60(1), 47-70.

Roof, W. (1996). *God is in the details: Reflections on religion's public presence in the United States in the mid-1990s.* Sociology of Religion, 57(2), 149-162.

Trenholm, S., & Jensen, A. (2000). *Interpersonal communication* (4th ed.). Belmont, CA: Wadsworth Publishing.

Wood, R. (1994). *Faith in action: Religious resources for political success in three congregations.* Sociology of Religion, 55(4), 397-417.

Wood, R. (1997). *Social capital and political culture: God meets politics in the inner city.* American Behavioral Scientist, 40(5), 595-605.

Chapter 9

Implications of Conceptualizations of Spirituality for Organizational Communication

Rachel M. Pokora
Nebraska Wesleyan University

Abstract

The study of organizational spirituality challenges scholars to re-think notions of organizing and cast a wider net when determining practices relevant to organizational communication. Different conceptualizations of spirituality offer organizational communication scholars unique insights into organizational practice. In this chapter I address differences between individual and organizational spirituality. I also present a typology of meanings of spirituality and address the implications of each for organizational communication. This chapter ends with a discussion on the role spirituality plays in organizational life and the challenge spirituality presents to organizational communication scholars.

The meaning of spirituality changes constantly (Chittister, 1998). In this essay I discuss briefly a typology of spirituality that consists of four categories of meanings of spirituality (Pokora 1996). These categories are *linking spirituality, path spirituality, incorporeal spirituality*, and *totalizing spirituality*. A person's understanding of spirituality may fit nicely into only one category of my typology; however, these categories are by no means mutually exclusive. In fact, it is possible for one's understanding of spirituality to include all four categories. I believe that this typology offers communication scholars a valuable framework to examine the implications of different meanings of spirituality.

Linking Spirituality and Path Spirituality

The first category I identify is *linking spirituality*, or that which links faith and action. This understanding of spirituality is manifest by a person who has a belief in God or some kind of higher power and puts her/his faith into action. The means by which that faith is put into action is spirituality. Chittister (1998) notes "spirituality is what we do because of what we say we believe rather than the pursuit of belief itself" (p. 15). For example, Timmerman (1992) notes:

> One could characterize the spiritual life as the conversation, sometimes interrupted, sometimes lively, but always ongoing with that Unknown with which the known is connected. It is what we reach for when, in music or art or love or sport or work, we aim for more. Spirituality is the response of the whole person, body, mind, feelings, relationships, to the perceived presence of the holy in the here and now (p. 84).

For Timmerman, the action is a "response" to the holy. This response is the lived experience of spirituality. In the organizational realm, then, an attempt to work to one's full potential or to enact the will of God in the workplace are examples of linking spirituality.

Another example of linking spirituality is Gustavo Gutierrez's *Liberation Theology*. Gutierrez (1984) grounds spirituality in lived experience and considers these lived experiences of spirituality to be encounters with God. Gutierrez contrasts his understanding of spirituality with isolationist spiritualities or spiritualities whose sole focus is God at the expense of other individuals or the community in which we live. For Gutierrez, prayer and action should be linked in such a way that one views his/her responsibility to others as part of his/her spirituality. In this way, people who attempt to better the lives of others through their work, if it is grounded in their faith lives, exhibit linking spirituality in their organizations.   In addition, organizations whose missions include philanthropy rooted in faith can be said to have a spirituality.

The second category of spirituality which is manifest in observable ways is *path spirituality*.   Path spirituality offers specific practices designed to help one experience or develop a closer relationship with the divine.   Often these practices are connected with specific religious denominations or formal groups affiliated with specific religions.   For example, within the Roman Catholic Church, many religious orders follow a specific path toward holiness.   There are Franciscan, Benedictine, and Carmelite spiritualities.   Manifestations of path spirituality reach far beyond vowed religious communities, however.   Meditation techniques, fasting, and even prayers said before class in parochial schools are examples of path spirituality.

Conceptualizing spirituality as a path can be useful for organizational communication scholars who wish to focus on that which is specific and observable such as organizational storytelling or other manifestations of organizational culture.   As groups of people share a path in an attempt to experience/draw closer to the divine, they can share the stories of their journeys, rites and rituals, etc.   These journeys become part of an organization's culture and have direct implications on how and why people act, or do not act, in certain ways in the organization.

These two categories of spirituality, linking and path, are the most easily observed because they can be tied to specific organizational practices and behaviors.   A focus on these two categories allows organizational communication scholars to focus on actual behaviors that construct organizations and allows us to illuminate the impact of spirituality on organizational life.

Incorporeal Spirituality and Totalizing Spirituality

I turn now to the last two categories of spirituality, *incorporeal and totalizing*.   While both linking and path spiritualities could be observed and measured by an organizational communication scholar, these two categories raise more complicated issues.   They challenge us to consider new ways of thinking about being human in organizations.

Incorporeal spirituality can be understood as that which is separate from matter.   In this understanding, spirituality is linked with "things of the spirit" (Jones, Wainwright, & Yarnold, 1986, p. xxiv).   This is a basic understanding of spirituality and the definition that can be found in the dictionary. The Random House Dictionary (1988) defines spirit as "the incorporeal part of man [sic] in general or of an individual, or an aspect of this, such as the mind or soul." In this definition, "spirit" can be individual or communal. Spiritual is defined as "of, pertaining to, or consisting of spirit; incorporeal." Describing humans as spiritual beings means they have spirits. Similarly, a spiritual collective has communal spirit. Spirituality, then, is defined as "the quality or fact of being spiritual." Or, as Chinnici (1985) notes, spirituality is "life in the spirit" (p. viii).

In contrast to incorporeal spirituality, *totalizing spirituality* reflects the belief that everything is spirituality, including the material. As Schneiders (1989) notes, "the term [spirituality] has broadened to connote the whole of the life of faith and even the life of the person as a whole including its bodily, psychological, social, and political dimensions" (p. 679). Capra and Steindle-Rast (1991) explain that "spirituality lets Religion flow into your eating, into your writing, into clipping your fingernails" (p. 13). Because spirituality pervades our beings, it cannot be separated from our actions, thoughts, or our selves. Therefore, spirituality affects and is affected by every other aspect of our lives.

This postmodern world of fragmentation can be a lonely place as we focus on how we are different from one another. A view of spirituality as incorporeal and/or totalizing offers a way that humans (or all living beings, in some spiritualities) are connected with one another. Goodall refers to a type of connection he calls "interbeing" (1993, p. 40). The concept of interbeing was discussed by a Vietnamese monk, Thich Nhat Hanh. Interbeing "refer[s] to the spiritual interconnectedness of every entity in the cosmos" (Goodall, 1993, p. 43). Some argue that all life is connected by a consciousness which few have even begun to tap. If an organizational communication scholar studies spirituality with this understanding, s/he can focus on what connects humans and bridges the gap that language and exclusivity of experience creates. As Goodall (1993) notes, "We have severely limited what 'counts' as communicative experiences to those that can be merely observed instead of those undeniably communicative experiences that are sensed, felt, or mediated by the ineffable. Yet how strange this absence is" (p. 46). In other words, Goodall believes that we should treat spirituality as communication. This connection might be made through Victor Turner's idea of "communitas" (Turner & Turner, 1978). Communitas is "a relational quality of full unmediated communication, even communion, between definite and determinate identities, which arises spontaneously in all kinds of groups, situations, and circumstances" (p. 250). In this sense, spirituality as communication is transcendent.

Conclusion

The non-material has direct implications on how organizational members create and re-create organizational life. We therefore need to develop a way to talk about the way that non-material notions can be incorporated in our theories of organizational communication.

In other words, if we intend to theorize about spirituality and organizational life, one of our first tasks is to struggle with and negotiate the different meanings of spirituality that come with organizational life. I believe that the typology I offer in this essay helps us with this task.

Chapter 10

African American Women and Spirituality Advancing Our Understanding of Leadership and Organizing

Patricia S. Hill
University of Akron

Abstract

The focus of this chapter is on the leadership roles of African American women in religious and spiritual communities. I explore the role of religion and spirituality in the lives of African American women toward understanding how structures of religious institutions and gender oppression have impacted women's involvement in spiritual leadership and their own spiritual identities.

The positive ramifications of religious beliefs and spirituality in the lives of African American women have been well established (Chatters, Levin & Taylor, 1992; Collier-Thomas, 1998; Collins, 1998, 1990; Cone & Wilmore, 1993; Ellison, 1983; McKay, 1989, Murray, 1993; Stewart, 1995). Much literature reveals long secular traditions that inform African American women's day-to-day efforts to use their spiritual and religious convictions to forge their own self-definitions as well as meaningful understandings of gender, family and community (Bushnell, 1980; Collier-Thomas, 1998; Grant; 1989; Nunnally-Cox, 1981; Weems, 1988). Moreover, African American women's history reveals a recognition of spirituality and faith as a "moral and ethical system of African American culture that was central to survival as well as wholeness and healing" (Hine & Thompson, 1998, p. 18). While much attention has been given to recognition of the importance of religion and spirituality in the life of African American women, much less has been written about African American women's importance in the life of church and spiritual organizations, specifically in terms of leadership building.

Several scholars have argued that African American religious and spiritual organizations have been problematic for African American women's leadership in that they foster social control through their patriarchal structures and androcentric practices (Andersen, 1998; Bushnell, 1980; Cannon, 1995; hooks, 1991; Weems, 1988). Andersen (1998) maintains that religion is a powerful source for the subordination of African American women in contemporary society because African American religious beliefs are at the core of sexist ideologies that promote women's exclusion from religious leadership and maintain women's subordination in the home. She states that:

> the church has historically provided the basis for the double standard of male and female sexuality. Women's role models in the church are defined through women's sexual behavior and dichotomize women in two polars: Eve, the temptress, and Mary, the virginal mother. (p. 2)

Collier-Thomas (1998, p. 33) posits that "many clergymen [sic] still use biblical references to assert the inferiority of women" and to reinforce patriarchal structures and traditional role expectations. She writes:

> The most often quoted biblical source is the Apostle Paul, who wrote the "Women should be silent in the churches' (1 Cor. 14:34) and 'I do not permit a woman to teach or have authority over an man" (1 Tim. 2:12).

Hayes (1996) observes that it has only been recently, within the last fifteen or so years, that African American women have become part of religious and spiritual leadership. She notes that:

> Black women have held few significant roles of responsibility or leadership within [church traditions], especially as ordained ministers. Those who did have such roles, few as they were, were constantly challenged by both men and women as to the propriety of their roles, their ability to fulfill them, and the validity of their calling. (p. 31)

In mainstream society, leadership is concentrated in the hands of those who have been able through appointment, election, effort, credibility or mere fortune to take command of institutions that control and distribute valuable resources (Barge, 1994; Dobbins & Zaccaro, 1986; Feidler, 1967; Shockley-Zalabak, 1994). Androcentric theology and practices have rendered invisible the leadership experiences of women because much scholarship has defined religious leadership as singularly male in character and composition (Cannon, 1995). Higgenbotham (1993) argues that the religious and spiritual leadership of women has been dismissed and disregarded on the premise that women have no "historical presence, theological insight, or noteworthy influence" (p. 141). These assumptions are particularly problematic for African American women's theology, Collins (1990) maintains, because such a theology is situated at the intersection of race, class and gender oppression, which is inextricably interwoven in the racial history of domination and subordination. To understand African American women and their development as religious and spiritual leaders, I therefore believe that it is useful to explore how, in the midst of exclusion and sexist church and spiritual traditions and practices, they have been able to forge a path toward their own recognition and empowerment.

Religious Traditions as Empowerment

Yet several scholars recognize that while religious ideology is a powerful source for the subordination of women in society, it has also been an important source for the feminist movement and other social political movements for human liberation (Andersen 1998; Collier-Thomas 1998; Gilkes, 1990; Grant, 1989). This is particularly evident in many African American communities where religion has been a stable force of empowerment (Cone & Wilmore, 1993). According to Hine and Thompson (1998), the Black church has historically served as a solid institution for group cohesion and solidarity. The Black church offered security, reassurance, a promise for salvation in the afterlife, and it symbolized freedom. The Black church was and continues to be a focal point of African American community life. For many African American women, it has played a key role in education, social control, economic development, and recreation, which all contributed toward the advance of the race.

Despite the absence of their vision, and the stifling of their distinct legacy when church history is memorized, African American women have built a space for their own recognition in Black religious organizations in ways that didn't require traditions sacred to maleness or whiteness. In spite of all the macro-social systems of social inequality, African American women forged ahead, preaching and teaching and "determined to pursue a leadership ordained by God himself" (Collier-Thomas, 1998, p. 35). They transcended boundaries and created new leadership traditions with their involvement and dedication in organizing programs designed to raise consciousness. Gilkes (1990) suggests that these traditions have been highly sustaining for African American women by providing a community that not only offered interpretations other than those put forth by dominant society, but also creating safe spaces in which to develop leadership skills.

The reality is that legions of African American women have preached for almost two hundred years, and spiritual leadership continues to be of primary importance for many African American women. Hayes (1996) maintains that the problem of sexism is slowly changing in many churches and faith organizations in African American communities, as women continue to enter programs of theological study in ever increasing numbers. Moreover, African American women are creating theological norms that are in harmony with social justice in their embrace of women-centered theological models such as Womanist theology.

Womanist Theology

Alice Walker coined the term Womanist in her 1983 essay collection, *In Search of Our Mother's Gardens*. According to Walker, a Womanist is committed to survival and wholeness of an entire people, male and female and is opposed to separation. She is wanting to know more and in greater depth than is good for one . . . [She is] outrageous, audacious, courageous and engages in willful behavior. A Womanist is universal, encompassing love for men and women as well as the Spirit and herself, "regardless". (Walker, 1983, p. 18)

To foster visibility of African American women in leadership roles, Womanist theology has emerged. Employing Walker's definition of Womanist, African American women are calling into question their suppressed role in African American churches and faith communities. Womanist theology is both theory and practice of inclusivity, accenting gender, race, class, and sexual orientation. Because of its inclusive conceptual framework, Womanist theology exemplifies reconstructed knowledge beyond the monovocal concerns of dominant theology. The emergence of Womanist theology presents possibilities for rewriting religious and spiritual traditions in a way that speaks to the complexities, sensibilities, and uniqueness of women's experiences. As a result, Womanist theology is reconstructing new knowledge.

Informed by these assumptions, Womanist theologians bring to the center the experience and knowledge of those marginalized by complex layering of race, gender, and class oppression. This creates a space for the claiming of experiences of African American women and their contributions to history. Moreover, it allows for interpretation of what these experiences mean in relation to God and spirituality.

Womanist theology assumes a liberatory perspective so that African American women can live embolden lives within their communities and within the larger society. It advances a leadership style informed by a framework that allows women to "talk back" (hooks, 1991) to structures and ideology that oppress, thereby maintaining spaces and spheres for women to exercise their spiritual gifts and leadership.

Conclusion

The presence of African American women in leadership roles takes on highly significant meanings in religious organizational life. Religious traditions and faith communities have tended to neglect the spirituality of African American women by legitimating the value of other structures whose spiritual values may be based on power relationships.

African American women who provide spiritual leadership have not been as scarce as the literature on women, religion, and African American experiences suggests. Although women who preach and provide spiritual leadership have not been, and still are, not widely recognized in mainstream religious organizations as the equals of their male counterparts, they have continued to come forth and to be empowered in leadership roles and theological discourse. In doing so, they present a strong rebuttal to the depiction of African American women as "temptress or virginal" or as spiritually inferior.

The leadership and organizing efforts of African American women serve as a repository for knowledge. Current literature on African American spiritual leadership highlights the enduring traditions of African American women's use of spiritual and religious convictions to forge their own self-definitions and leadership. The continued study of the spiritual lives of African American women holds the promise of elucidating the role between spiritual identities and spiritual leadership. As a result, it is crucial to our understanding of organizations. Without examining such experiences, and acknowledging the opportunities they present for women everywhere, we cannot hope to change hegemony in sacred and secular organizations.

References

Andersen, M. L. (1998). *Thinking about women: Sociological perspectives on sex and gender.* Boston: Allyn and Bacon.

Barge, J. K. (1994). *Leadership: Communication skills for organizations and groups.* New York: St. Martin's Press.

Brown-Douglas, K. (1993). A trouble in my soul. In J. H. Cone & G. S. Wilmore (Eds.), *Black Theology (I)* (pp. 209-299). Maryknoll, NY: Orbis Books.

Bushnell, K, C. (1980). *God's word to women: One hundred Bible studies on women's place in the divine economy.* North Collins, NY: Munson.

Cannon, K. G. (1988) *Black Womanist ethics.* Atlanta, GA: Scholars Press.

Cannon, K. G. (1995). *Katie's Cannon: Womanism and the soul of the Black community.* New York: Continuum.

Chatters, L., Levin, J. & Taylor, R. J. (1992). Antecedents and dimensions of religious involvement among older Black adults. *Journal of Gerontology, 47,* 269-278.

Collier, Thomas, B. (1998). *Daughters of thunder: Black women preachers and their sermons 1850-1979.* San Francisco: Jossey-Bass.

Collins, P. H. (1990). *Black feminist thought: Knowledge, consciousness, and the politics of empowerment.* New York: Routledge.

Collins, P. H. (1998). *Fighting words: Black women and the search for justice.* Minneapolis, MN: University of Minnesota Press.

Cone, J. H. & Wilmore, G. S. (1993) *Black Theology: A documentary history (II) 1980-1992.* Maryknoll: NY: Orbis.

Dobbins, G. H., & Zaccaro, S. J. (1986). The effects of group cohesion and leader behavior on subordinate satisfaction. *Group and Organization Studies, 11,* 203-319.

Ellison, C. (1983). Spiritual well-being: Conceptualization and measurement. *Journal of Psychology and Theology, 4,* 330-340.

Feidler, F. (1967). *A theory of leadership effectiveness.* New York: McGraw-Hill.

Gilkes, C. T. (1990). Together and in harness: Women's tradition in the sanctified Church. In M. R. Malson, E Mudimbe-Boyi, Jean F. O'Barr, and Mary Wyer (Eds.) *Black women in America: Social science perspectives* (pp. 229-244). Chicago: University of Chicago Press.

Grant, J. (1989). *White women's Christ and Black women's Jesus: Feminist Christology and Womanist response.* Atlanta: Scholars Press.

Hayes, D. L . (1996). *And still we rise : An introduction to Black liberation theology.* New York : Paulist Press.

Higgenbotham, E. B. (1993). *Righteous discontent: The women's movement in the Black Baptist Church.* Cambridge: Harvard University Press.

Hine, D. C. & Thompson, K. (1998). *A shining thread of hope.* New York: Broadway Books.

hooks, b. (1991) *Ain't I a woman: Black women and feminism.* Boston: South End Press.

Jewett, P. K. (1980). *The ordination of women.* Grand Rapids, MI: Erdman's Press.

McKay, N. Y. (1989). Nineteenth-century Black women's spiritual autobiographies: Religious faith and self-empowerment. In Personal Narrative Group (Eds.). *Interpreting women's lives: Feminist theory and personal narrative.* Bloomington: Indiana University Press.

Murray, P. (1993) Black Theology and Feminist Theology: A Comparative View. In J. H. Cone & G. S. Wilmore (Eds.), *Black Theology: A documentary History, 1966-1979 Vol. I,* (pp. 304-402). Maryknoll: NY: Orbis.

Nunnally-Cox, J. (1981). *Foremothers: Women of the Bible.* New York: Seabury Press.

Shockley-Zalabak, P. (1994). *Understanding organizational communication: Cases, commentaries, and conversations.* White Plans, NY: Longman.

Stewart, M. W. (1995). O, ye daughters of Africa, awake! In B. Guy-Shaftall (Ed.) *Words of Fire: an anthology of African American Feminist Thought.* (pp.202-244). New York: The New Press.

Walker, A. (1983). *In search of our mother's gardens: Womanist Prose.* New York: Harvest.

Weems, R. J. (1988). *Just a sister away: A Womanist vision of women's relationships in the Bible.* San Diego: Laura Media.

Chapter 11

On the Spiritual Nature of Communication

Amardo Rodriguez
Syracuse University

Abstract

This essay pushes forward a spiritual understanding of communication (Rodriguez, 2001). I contend that human beings possess a set of strivings that uniquely give us the ability to construct deep and complex relations with the world. Our proclivity and capacity for meaning creation is such a striving. In this essay, spirituality reflects our striving to establish communion with the cosmos. I discuss briefly how a spiritual understanding of communication expands our understanding of what being human means and gives communication theorists and teachers a new ontological position to look anew at communication.

A cursory look at communication journals and popular communication texts rarely finds mention of scholarly work that rests on spiritual assumptions. It is difficult to find any claim that communication is a spiritual phenomenon that reflects spiritual beings. Tukey (1990) contends that communication theorists "consider no dimension other than the mental, social and biological—in short, only the secular. What contemporary theories ignore is human spirituality and its possible role in human communication" (p. 66). We have, as Smith (1993) notes, "assiduously [avoided] talking about the non-material elements of communication" (p. 267). Indeed, a secular hegemony pervades communication theory and inquiry that circumscribes certain notions about what being human means, our relations to each other, and our relation to the world.

This essay pushes forward a spiritual understanding of communication (Rodriguez, 2001). Attention to the spiritual dimension of being human enlivens the potential of communication theory to deepen our understanding of what being human means in many important ways. Increasingly, scholars are calling attention to the spiritual element of communication (e.g., Chase, 1993; Goodall, 1993; Kirkwood, 1993; McPhail, 1996; Ohlhauser, 1996; Rodriguez, 2001; Tukey, 1990). The recently created Spiritual Communication Commission within the National Communication Association is born out of this call. According to Smith (1993), "The problem with ignoring the spiritual is that we cannot deepen our theory nor advance our understanding of the art of rhetoric without investigating the spiritual dimension"(p. 268). Chase (1993) writes, "Rethinking human communication by recognizing the fundamental experience of obligation for the Other provides an exciting framework by which one can challenge the recurring . . . practices of everyday life which produce and reproduce a disregard for the social, material, and spiritual well-being of people, as well as a disregard for the service due a transcendent Spiritual Being" (p. 14). Long (1997) believes that a spiritual perspective "with regard to communication research allows us to go beyond the transmission mode of communicating to re-embody a more complex knowing and relationships with others and ourselves" (pp. 9-10).

Theorists are increasingly calling attention to spirituality in our study of the human condition. This call recognizes that spirituality challenges dominant ontological and epistemological assumptions. For example, Lindsay (1998) writes:

> Spirituality should not be considered a residual to mainstream

experience. It is not just the unimportant detail that is unexplained by science. Just because most of science . . . has missed explaining the key nature of the universe does not mean that it is the residual. Too often science studies the accessible, not the important. To resign the inaccessible (through scientific method) to the residual, is to miss the point. (p. 1)

Different definitions of spirituality appear in this emerging spiritual thrust in the academy. For Lyles (1998), "Spirituality is about the courage to evolve beyond the simple, the animal, in us. It is about holding oneself and others accountable to higher standards of behavior" (p.1). Moreover, "Our spirituality must be critical and analytical and highly demanding of human action within organizations" (p. 1). Jacques (1998) views spirituality as "a context of wonder" (p. 1). According to Lindsay (1998):

> Spirituality is the art of breaking through the illusion. It is the experience of nonordinary reality in ordinary life. It is touching the life that is everything. It is dropping our species-centrism to become one with animals. It is the ultimate journey to the self and the ultimate journey to the other. It is living in balance and respect with other life forms and the earth. It is the deep knowing of ancestors that lives in our genes. It is the higher knowledge of spirit and the void of creation. It is the journey to yourself as you could be. It holds the healing for your wounds and the meaning for your quest. (p. 1)

Yet communication theory and inquiry reflect an understanding of communication that is highly secular in origin. In most cases, communication is understood as an artifact of being (Rodriguez, 2001). That is, human beings are assumed to have no spiritual striving that communication constitutes. We assume that the origins of communication reside in necessity and utility. For example, in an essay entitled *Communication, Conflict, and Culture*, Mortensen posits that language, culture, and communication coevolved to end the violent conflict that is of our endowed capacity for strife and conflict. According to Mortensen (1991), "Struggle and strife permeate relations between human beings in ways that are peculiar to the species" (p. 275). No doubt, the secular hegemony that pervades extant communication theory imposes a certain cultural and political worldview. It subtly suppresses other understandings of communication, other ways of understanding and experiencing the world. This hegemony determines what research interests are interesting, valid, and worthy of support. In fact, this secular hegemony privileges a certain cultural, political, and racial worldview. It represents a pernicious kind of colonialism.

An understanding of communication that rests on spiritual assumptions brings a new set of ontological and epistemological assumptions to communication.   It expands our understanding of communication and, in so doing, expands our understanding of what being human means. Indeed, whereas so much of communication scholarship is concerned with describing communication behavior and processes, such as cognition processes, gender differences and communication styles, cultural differences and communication behavior, conflict styles and negotiation tactics, and so forth, a spiritual understanding of communication foregrounds the human element. It is fundamentally concerned with how communication expands our understanding of what being human means. The reason being that communication is seen as the constitutive element of being human.   Communication uniquely defines us.   Through communication, that is, through our striving for meaning creation, we uniquely possess the capacity to forge deep and complex relations with the world and each other.

A spiritual understanding of communication draws our attention to our condition with the world and each other, and the types of communicative and performative practices that either hinder or foster our forging deep and complex relations.   A spiritual understanding of communication inherently brings a moral foundation to communication theory and inquiry.   Our communicative and performative practices bear on the condition of the world and the humanity of others. In this regard, a spiritual view of communication in no way depolitiicizes the study of communication.   In fact, such a view most politicizes the study of communication as the consequences and implications of our ways of being in the world in the widest and most perilous context. To be human is to have a moral responsibility for the condition of the world and each other. We are obligated to foster ways of being that affirm life, which is to say ways of being that promote love and compassion. A spiritual view of communication therefore also gives us a moral calculus.

A spiritual understanding of communication accents the commonality of the human condition without downplaying the differences that come with different cultures (Rodriguez, 2001).   Such an understanding foregrounds communication as a moral, existential, and spiritual striving. Communication, again, uniquely defines us. Further, communication is both cultural and universal. It is cultural from the standpoint that meanings always reflect and belong to different perspectives of being in the world. Meanings are perspectival and relational. On the other hand, communication is universal from the standpoint that our spiritual questing for new meanings pushes against local perspectives. Communication places and displaces us. It simultaneously gives us an understanding of the world and undercuts that understanding of the world. We can never mirror our experiences or our thoughts. Each retelling creates new experiences, new meanings, new understandings, and, eventually, new truths. Communication enables us by affording us constant access to new experiences, new meanings, and so on. No set of meanings, perspectives, or cultures can ever be permanently held constant and neither should we try to do so. The natural forces of the world disallow such ambitions.

The point is that the secular hegemony that pervades communication theory and inquiry limits our understanding of what being human means by assuming that human beings are aspiritual beings. Delegitimizing this hegemony demands perspectives of communication that embody a different set of ontological and epistemological assumptions. As Audre Lorde astutely observed, "The master's tools will never dismantle the master's house." Understandings of communication premised on spiritual assumptions give us new tools to build new understandings of what being human means. To assume that communication uniquely gives us the ability to construct deep and complex relations with the world is to believe that communication theory possesses a tremendous potentiality to speak to the condition of the world. A spiritual view of communication therefore enlivens communication theory and inquiry by bringing a deep urgency to the study of communication.

References

Chase, K. R. (1993). A spiritual and critical revision of structuration theory. *Journal of Communication and Religion, 16,* 1-21.

Goodall, H. L., Jr. (1993). Mysteries of the future told: Communication as the material manifestation of spirituality. *World Communication Journal, 22,* 40-49.

Jacques, R. (1995). Spirituality and residualism. *Electronic Journal of Radical Organizational Theory, 1 (I).*

Kirkwood, W. B. (1993). Studying communication about spirituality and the spiritual consequences of communication. *Journal of Communication and Religion, 17,* 13-26.

Lindsay, C. (1995). On spirituality as a residual. *Electronic Journal of Radical Organizational Theory, 1 (I).*

Long, K. L. (1997). *Sparring with Spirituality: Issues of entangling spirituality and communication.* Paper presented at the National Communication Association annual conference in Chicago, IL. November, 23-26.

Lyles, C. Y. (1995). On spirituality, residualism, and work. *Electronic Journal of Radical Organizational Theory, 1 (I).*

McPhail, M. L. (1996). Spirituality and the critique of epistemic rhetoric: A coherent analysis. *Journal of Communication and Religion, 19,* 48-60.

Mortensen, C. D. (1991). Communication, conflict, and culture. *Communication Theory, 4,* 273-293.

Ohlhauser, J. B. (1996). Human rhetoric: Accounting for spiritual intervention. *Howard Journal of Communications, 7,* 339-348.

Rodriguez, A. (2001). *On matters of liberation (I): The case against hierarchy.* Cresskill, NJ: Hampton.

Smith, C. R. (1993). Finding the spiritual dimension of rhetoric. *Western Journal of Communication, 57,* 266-271.

Tukey, D. (1990). Toward a research agenda for spiritual rhetoric. *Journal of Communication and Religion, 13,* 66-76.

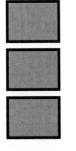

Hot Folder User

Document Name: 1115txt.pdf
Printing Time: 08/18/13 15:38:15
Copies Requested: 7
Account:
Virtual Printer: Nuvera-03/Nuvera3_small4up
Printed For: